an illustrated introduction to
THE SOMME 1916

Robert J. Parker

This book is dedicated to my great-uncle and namesake,
Pte Robert John Parker of the South Wales Border Regiment,
who served on the Somme sector as a stretcher-bearer.
Thanks also to my beloved wife Sheila.

Photo above courtesy of Annette Wood, Pte Parker's granddaughter.

Battle and trench plans by Thomas Bohm,
User Design, Illustration and Typesetting.

First published 2016

Amberley Publishing
The Hill, Stroud
Gloucestershire, GL5 4EP

www.amberley-books.com

British Library Cataloguing in Publication Data.
A catalogue record for this book is available from the British Library.

ISBN 978 1 4456 4442 4 (paperback)
ISBN 978 1 4456 4520 9 (ebook)

Typesetting and Origination by Amberley Publishing.
Printed in Great Britain.

CONTENTS

	The Battle of the Somme in Five Minutes	5
	Timeline	9
1	Impact of the Battle of the Somme	13
2	Causes of the First World War	17
3	Pre-Somme Situation	21
4	Preparation	36
5	Supplies and Transport	50
6	1 July 1916: The First Day	57
7	The Next Four Months	65
8	Technological Innovations	71
9	The End of the Battle	78
10	Conclusions	80
11	Analysis	87
	What Next?	93
	Notes	94
	Index	95

THE BATTLE OF
THE SOMME IN FIVE MINUTES

1 July 1916: A date that has become legendary in the annals of British and world history. The Battle of the Somme began with a week-long preliminary bombardment expending over 1.5 *million* artillery shells, followed by an assault of over 100,000 soldiers along a nearly 20-mile front in Picardy, France. It was the prelude to more than four months of human slaughter that would witness over one million British, French and German casualties and gain virtually nothing in terms of tactical, strategic or geographical value. It was the Battle of the Somme.

The Battle of the Somme was an event of enormous proportions. The sheer number of soldiers engaged, the massive logistical support required, the extent and depth of planning and preparation, the mountains of material requirements, the duration, geographical breadth, cost and result all rank it as one of the largest battles in world history. Its significance and impact during and after the war has only increased, placing it statistically and historically as a watershed in military, social and political importance. The legacy of the Battle of the Somme poses the ultimate philosophical and military question: when is a piece of territory (or strategic objective) no longer worth the cost of seizing it? To what extremes should human endeavour and investment be risked in order to achieve a perceived goal? Can the sacrifice in blood and treasure be justified for the sake of the desired objective? And, ultimately, when is too much truly too much?

The Battle of the Somme is the climax of these questions and facts. The numbers alone speak volumes. Attacking for four and a half months along a 15- to 20-mile front, the allied Anglo-French forces presented a combined assault of more than twenty divisions comprising nearly a quarter of a million men, two-thirds of

Opposite: Enlistment posters encouraging volunteers for the British Army, and featuring the imposing image of Lord Horatio Kitchener urging young men to enlist for king and country. Eventually, the government would be forced to use conscription to fill the depleted ranks. (Library of Congress)

these being British. A similarly large German army stood poised to receive this attack, although the German defenders would be sheltered in deeply protected bunkers and in rearguard positions. The British would use a week's preparation of heavy artillery bombardment to soften up the German defences. The plan was to demolish entangling barbed wire and kill as many German defenders as possible, to ultimately allow roughly 150,000 heavily laden infantrymen to casually cross the 'no man's land' between the British and German positions and seize the destroyed German positions with little or no expected resistance. They would then continue forward with a breakthrough to the rear of the German lines. In reality, the British Army suffered its deadliest day in history. On the first day of battle alone, it suffered nearly 60,000 casualties; of these, nearly 20,000 would be killed. 1 July 1916 would go down as one of the greatest single days of human slaughter in military history. The battle continued day after day until mid-November when the weather and appalling losses, coupled with little or no territorial or strategic gain, finally brought attacks to a halt. Though the numbers are disputed, it is safe to say that the British alone suffered approximately 400,000–450,000 casualties during the nearly five-month battle; the French another 150,000–200,000; and the Germans a comparable 450,000–500,000.

In the process, a gain of perhaps 5 miles of front was accomplished. Certainly the intended breakthrough failed. From this failure and previous failed attacks came the proclaimed strategy of attrition, whereby horrific losses without visible battlefield gain or success would be marked as contributing to the overall defeat of the German army through the process of wearing it down in numbers, equipment and morale. For many, this explanation became merely a hindsight justification for the bankrupt tactics and massive mortality numbers.

Controversial at the time in 1916, the Somme continues to generate fierce debate concerning its tactics and goals, human cost, brutally violent conduct, sacrificial nature and lack of any obvious tactical or strategic benefits. Following the Battle of the Somme, Britain replaced Herbert Asquith with David Lloyd George as Prime Minister, considered shifting its commanding officer Douglas Haig to another command, and pondered what its role in the First World War should be, and to what extreme should that participation be pursued. Even though it achieved victory in 1918, Great Britain would emerge as a radically different society, nation and empire.

Indeed, the world that existed before 1914 became irreversibly altered, politically, socially and geographically. Previously wealthy Great Britain became a debtor nation, especially to its economically robust ally, the United States.

Germany too was mired in deep debt, but also plagued by vicious political and social upheaval that would lead to the rise of Hitler and Nazism. The Russian Empire would collapse into violent revolution and civil war, leading to a virulent Bolshevik government in Russia. The Austro-Hungarian Empire would disintegrate into a handful of several weak and feuding independent states. The Ottoman Empire would also collapse in a similar manner in the Middle East. Today's world remains plagued by the convulsive rivalries of the nations that comprised much of the former Austrian, Russian and Ottoman Empires. Great Britain would witness the challenges of labour and social unrest, and economically all of Europe and the industrialised world would experience the debacle of the Great Depression, only to be 'relieved' through the excruciating agony and catastrophic havoc of the Second World War – the ultimate child of the First World War.

The Battle of the Somme reflects the scale and tragedy of the First World War. It underscores the courage, carnage and cost of the war as fought by the British Army on the Western Front. It is the full representation of the desire, tempered by the frustration, of Britain's political and military leaders to come to grips with an industrialised war that had evolved into an all-devouring monster of unprecedented size and appetite. The battle reflected the conundrum of how to wage a new form of warfare while coping with the question: to what length was Britain prepared to go in achieving its perceived goal? And ultimately: what were those goals and were they worth the significant sacrifices that were incurred?

Tyne Cot cemetery, the largest British and Commonwealth military cemetery in the world. It is located near the Ypres battlefield in Zonnebeek, Belgium. Immediately following the war, numerous cemeteries, memorials, and monuments were constructed to commemorate the dead. (Author's collection)

TIMELINE

- **1870–71**
  Franco-Prussian War. France suffers a humiliating defeat to Prussia. With Prussia at its core, the newly formed German Empire is born – modern-day Germany.

- **1882**
  The Triple Alliance between Germany, Austria-Hungary and Italy is formed (Italy later switches sides and joins the 'Allies').

- **1888**
  Wilhelm II becomes Kaiser (emperor) of Germany.

- **1907**
  Russia and Great Britain sign an agreement that virtually allies the nations of Russia, France and Great Britain (the Triple Entente) against the powers of the Triple Alliance.

- **28 June 1914**
  Archduke Franz Ferdinand of Austria is assassinated in Sarajevo, Bosnia.

- **August 1914**
  War is declared between the rival allied groups containing Germany and Austria-Hungary (the Central Powers) and France and Russia. Belgium is invaded by Germany and Great Britain sends its Expeditionary Force (BEF) to France under General Sir John French, forming the 'Allies'.

- **December 1915**
  British General Sir John French is replaced by General Sir Douglas Haig, who will command the BEF until the end of the war.

- **December 1915**
  A conference at Chantilly, France, is held by the 'Allies' calling for a large Russian attack on the Eastern Front (the Brusilov Offensive) and a large combined Franco-British attack on the Western Front along the Somme River in France.

- **February 1916**
  The Germans launch the Battle of Verdun in north-eastern France, placing a severe strain on the French ability to continue the war and increasing the necessity for the Somme offensive to relieve pressure on French forces. Verdun would continue until December of 1916.

- **June 1916**

  Heavy artillery bombardment of German positions, a prelude to the attacks; over one million shells fired upon the German defences in preparation for the assault.

- **1 July 1916**

  The Somme Offensive begins. The single most deadly day in British military history. Nearly 60,000 British casualties and nearly 20,000 British soldiers killed on 'Day One' alone. Due to the extreme commitments of the French at Verdun, the Somme offensive evolves into a largely British operation.

Battle of the Somme: First Phase

- **1–13 July**

  Battle of Albert. British and French forces secure several objectives: French towns of Montauban, Fricourt and Mametz. Most objectives, however, remain unsecured including Day One objectives of the French towns of Bapaume and Peronne. A major breakthrough on the Western Front does not occur.

- **14–20 July**

  Battles of Bazintine Ridge and Fromelles: British assaults fail to secure objectives of the heavily defended German position, the Schwaben Redoubt, or the French towns of Thiepval and Pozières. German resistance and counter-attacks are heavy and relentless. At Fromelles the Australians incur heavy losses.

Battle of the Somme: Second Phase

- **14 July – 15 September**

  Battle of Delville Wood. British attempt to secure their right flank in order to gain Pozières Ridge.

- **23 July – 7 August**

  Battle of Pozières Ridge. Lengthy, concurrent and difficult assaults, but over the summer both are eventually successful. Gains are small and at great cost in casualties. Australians succeed in taking the Pozières position.

- **3–9 September**

  Battles of Guillemont and Ginchy. British continue to make marginal gains. September witnesses heaviest month of German losses at the Somme.

Battle of the Somme: Third Phase

- **15–28 September**

  Battles of Flers and Morval. Village of Flers is taken with the first successful use of tanks to capture a position.

- **26–28 September**

  Battle of Thiepval. After almost three months of bitter fighting, the Thiepval Heights and Schwaben Redoubt (14 October) are finally captured. Both had been primary 1 July objectives.

- **1 October – 11 November**

  Battle of Ancre Heights. Another six weeks of intense fighting and worsening weather as the British finally succeed in capturing the commanding ridge over the village of Ancre. Also Battle of Transloy Heights. The objective is denied by foul weather and stubborn German resistance. Day One overall objectives of the French towns of Bapaume and Peronne remain in German hands.

- **13–18 November**

  Battle of Ancre. After four and a half months of savage fighting, Ancre remains under German control. General Haig calls for cessation of the offensive due to the onset of winter. The desired goal of a major breakthrough remains elusive.

- **18 November**

  The Battle of the Somme officially ends.

- **Winter 1916**

  Both armies dig in for winter. The following spring, the Germans fall back to a more defendable position, conceding the ground that the British and French spent nearly six months and 600,000 casualties to assault and the Germans nearly another 600,000 to defend.

- **April 1917**

  The United States declares war on Germany, and within a year begin swelling the Allied ranks with fresh soldiers and vast quantities of supplies.

- **March – April 1918**

  All-out bid by Germany in a spring offensive to win the war. It fails.

- **Summer – Autumn 1918**

  Allied counter-offensive. The Allies are now under the unified command of French general Ferdinand Foch. German army begins falling back toward Germany and surrendering in large numbers.

- **11 November 1918**

  The Armistice ends the fighting. Germany surrenders.

- **June 1919**

  Treaty of Versailles signed at the Paris Peace Conference, officially ending the First World War.

Remnants of the extensive trench system that stretched from the North Sea to the Swiss Alps are still visible to this day; this one is located on the Somme battlefield. (Author's collection)

1
IMPACT OF THE BATTLE OF THE SOMME

The First World War, referred to then as the 'Great War', was a war like no other that had gone before. Its size, carnage and ramifications dwarf the imagination and swamp attempts at adequate comprehension. Twenty short years later, a second and even greater cataclysmic global war would sweep the world, casting its vast shadow over the First World War. For decades the Second World War tended to relegate its predecessor to being widely overlooked and forgotten in terms of its historical scope and importance. But with the centenary anniversary and subsequent honouring of the First World War memory, the true significance, impact and repercussions of the war are being exhaustively re-examined and reconsidered. The result is a renewed respect for its ferocity, enormity and ultimate consequence to the world we have today.

To this day arguments rage as to the causes and necessity of this massive calamity. So too does the debate continue, as historians attempt to reveal a viable meaning for the depths reached in sheer killing and destruction of not just mortal men but of an age. Merging with this great debate is the resultant reminder of the tragic and undeniable lack of a lasting peace to emerge from such an immense conflagration, and the bitter fate of the world to endure an even greater and more deadly conflict – the Second World War. Adding to the First World War's immediate legacy and tragedy was the necessity to later erase the issues that were exposed and created, but left unresolved, by the First World War. The futility of the First World War's conclusion, coupled with its enormous expense in blood and treasure, remains a testament to a failed responsibility by those in positions of leadership. Wars are not necessarily inevitable; men make and fight wars, and the First World War was the supreme example of a vast sacrifice in lives, wealth and political stability. But to what end? Were the issues of 1914 great enough to support such an inferno of cost and consequence? Beyond the extraordinary investment in treasure and lives, and the political upheaval, there remained the unresolved and devastated social and governmental landscape that spawned the nightmare of the Second World War.

Herbert Asquith, British Prime Minister 1908–16. The Liberal PM was overwhelmed by the responsibilities and challenges of the First World War. The death of his son in the war further underscored his own personal tragedy and regret toward the conflict. He was replaced in late 1916 by David Lloyd George. Future Prime Minister Andrew Bonar Law would lose two sons, and former PM William Gladstone one, to the First World War. (Library of Congress, Bain Collection)

Within these great questions as to the cause and effect of the First World War, there resides the equally enduring and bitter controversy over how the war was fought. Due to its prodigious and unprecedented enormity, the methods, tactics and strategy of waging the First World War soon took on a dynamic of their own, a dynamic that consumed unparalleled quantities of men and means. Commanders struggled to find a path to victory while groping with the unprecedented capacity of an industrial lethality never before experienced or envisioned. The technological advances in weaponry had not been sufficiently recognised or matched by either the prudence of national leaders to hesitate before unleashing their armies of war, or by the tactical ability of their commanders to successfully develop a war of movement on the battlefield. The result was a stagnant war of attrition, feeding an insatiable appetite for physical, material and financial carnage. Unable to identify a method to achieve any recognizable battlefield gain or accomplishment, the stalemated war would be fought out until one side or the other became hopelessly exhausted, bled to death and financially broken. This became the result, as no practical solution evolved during the course of the war to break the stalemate. In so doing, a mindless consumption of men and material had to be endlessly fed into the savage demand of trench warfare before producing an endgame that enabled one side to ultimately achieve a condition of surrender and victory.

During the diabolical routine of trench warfare, there arose from time to time titanic battles that attempted to break the stalemate and achieve immediate victory. These mammoth efforts involved millions of men, months of preparation and planning, and

Winston Churchill with
Kaiser Wilhelm II of Germany
reviewing soldiers before
the First World War. They
would later become opposing
combatants. (Library of
Congress)

colossal amounts of material. All failed to achieve the goal of a breakthrough and accompanying victory; all resulted in tragically huge totals of casualties; and all are endlessly debated to this day for their seemingly distinct lack of imagination while stubbornly pursuing an implacable faith in potential success. The 1916 battles of Verdun and the Somme exemplify this obstinate mentality and stubbornness in the face of all reason for continuation. They have become the most famous examples of the futility, lethality and ferocity of the First World War. Both were strategically connected, both resulted in little or no gain over roughly six months of intense fighting, both witnessed outstanding sacrifices and examples of courage, and both saw nearly a million casualties with no obvious or identifiable accomplishment or gain.

To the British, the Battle of the Somme represents everything that the First World War was and was not. The Somme's human and financial cost, length, result and proximity to the United Kingdom (the pounding of the heavy guns could sometimes be heard in London), all tend to dramatise and underscore its significance, frustration and tragedy. It was the culmination of Great Britain's entry into the First World War. It would demonstrate Britain's capacity and determination to uphold its commitment to the Allied Alliance and promise to drive a wedge through the German lines to procure a tactical and strategic victory.

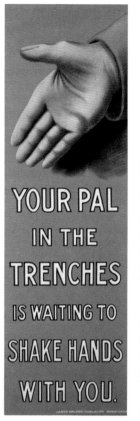

The tragic and poignant appeal for 'pals' volunteers. Fellow members of villages, factory shops, and sports clubs were encouraged to enlist and serve together. The campaign was successful and on 1 July many entire neighbourhood communities suffered the loss of entire groups of village 'pals' and 'chums'. (Library of Congress)

On a poignant note, the Somme battle featured a freshly recruited British volunteer army of over one million men. Many of the newly formed volunteer battalions were made up of 'pals', Secretary of State for War Lord Horatio Kitchener's grand design to increase enlistment. The scheme cleverly encouraged entire groups of young males from common villages, factories and shops to volunteer and serve alongside their fellow workers, neighbours and pub friends – and it succeeded. Tens of thousands signed on with their 'pals' to serve and fight with their mates. It would be a grand adventure and the Battle of the Somme would be the extension and result of this recruitment effort. Unfortunately, when a 'pals' battalion from a single village or factory came to be exposed to the horrific conditions at the Somme, the result could be especially devastating, as entire communities of young men would be killed – often in a single day. The Somme, with its catastrophic roll of casualties, remains a grim legacy that tragically resonates to this very day.

2
CAUSES OF
THE FIRST WORLD WAR

So why the Somme? Why was so immense an effort required during the First World War? Why, even, the First World War?

In the summer of 1914 Western Europe was by far the most prosperous and developed area in the world. Nations such as Germany, Great Britain and France had not only achieved financial wealth but were politically stable. Reaping the benefits of a generally peaceful environment, European nations prospered during a period of cultural development, economic vitality and overall confidence that had existed since the end of the Napoleonic Wars a century before. Although beginning to recognise the industrial and financial challenge of rapidly developing powers – most formidably the United States – Europe continued to control vast colonial empires that straddled the globe and continued to dominate the world economy. Very few could foresee a circumstance, let alone the desire, to engage upon a widespread war of self-destruction. While nations strenuously prepared their military might for such a conflict, it was assumed by most that no such contest would ever take place. To what possible purpose and to what end would such a war contribute?

There were, however, several incendiary issues that conceivably could ignite a war. Europe had witnessed and shrugged off minor wars in the nineteenth and early twentieth centuries, namely the Crimean War (1853–56) and several bitterly fought local wars in the Balkan Peninsula, but none of these had produced the type of catastrophe that the First World War was to become. And since it had not happened before, Europe's leaders were confident that a large continental war could not and would not happen in the future. Cooler heads would always prevail. This sense of supreme overconfidence was coupled with an ignorance of the possibility that events could slip out of their control. The toxic blend of naivety, arrogance and stupidity all nurtured a blind faith that everything would right itself – but instead it tragically mutated into the First World War. It was an event that should not have happened, but as Sir Edward Grey, British Foreign Secretary at the start of the war, prophetically proclaimed, 'the lights are going out all over Europe. We shall not see them lit again in our life-time.'[1] The path of the unpredictable would descend into the unimaginable.

Foremost of potential dangers was the division of Europe into two armed camps of interconnected allied groups, each promising to come to another's aid, even if its own self-interest was not threatened. The 'Triple Alliance' consisting of Germany, Austria-Hungary and Italy, confronted the 'Triple Entente' of France, Russia and the United Kingdom. Further confusing and endangering these major alliance groups were secondary commitments made by large nations to smaller and weaker ones. In particular was Russia's promise to aid Serbia, and Britain's pledge to come to the aid of Belgium. This network of alliances and promises would lead to a chain reaction of nations mobilising their armies (considered to be a declaration of war), actual declarations of war and foolish brinkmanship from which it would be difficult to back down. Nations placed their war-making apparatus in motion even though specific nations were neither openly threatened nor physically invaded.

Outbreaks of volatile and violent discontent criss-crossed Central and Southern Europe in the form of 'nationalist' political movements, in particular within the Austro-Hungarian Empire. The Balkan peninsula had already witnessed several minor wars and was a teeming cauldron of mixed religions, languages and ethnic groups all vying for their own political independence. It was a tinderbox of political and social upheaval. Attempting to harness and dominate this diverse region placed Austria-Hungary in a precarious position of governing an area that was fraught with potential violence, rebellion and revolution. Austria saw Serbia as the active promoter of these nationalistic tendencies. As they shared a predominantly Orthodox faith, Russia viewed herself as Serbia's defender to the larger and stronger Austro-Hungarian Empire. Austria's declaration of war against Serbia, followed by Russia's commitment to the defence of Serbia, was to trigger the eruption of the First World War.

Globally, the international competition for colonial empires and world trade was connected to wealth, prestige and envy. To Britain's chagrin, Germany was fast emerging as an industrial powerhouse, threatening Britain's status as the world's financial and economic leader. Further complicating the situation, Germany was rapidly building a modern and powerful navy that could potentially challenge Britain's control of the seas. The control of the seas was not only the heart of Britain's traditional military might, but also the lifeline to protecting and connecting Britain's far-flung empire and source of trade. Germany's emerging prowess on the high seas was perceived as a dangerous threat to Britain's military and economic position.

Hand in hand with Germany's aggressive naval build-up was Europe's heavy investment in weapons and armed service. Nations were training vast conscript armies with the capacity to mobilise, support and transport million-man armies rapidly and efficiently on a network of modern railroads. The weapons they now possessed were a paradigm leap in lethality. In particular, long-range artillery now used smokeless gunpowder of greater explosive power, able to hurl massive projectiles incredible distances – easily 5 to 10 miles with accuracy, and further in many instances. Rapid-firing machine guns could now spray bullets out of the barrel at astonishing rates of up to 600 rounds per minute.[2] Europe was armed to the teeth, heavily conscripted and industrially capable of mass-producing enormous quantities of guns, ammunition, military hardware, food and material to support armies of several million soldiers. If unleashed, the incredible potency, deadly firepower and capacity for massive annihilation of battlefield soldiers would be extreme–and virtually unanticipated. This unpredicted capability of introducing previously unseen magnitudes of destruction would overwhelm all manner of previous tactical and strategic experience.

Not to be ignored was Prussia's defeat of France in the Franco-Prussian War of 1870–71 and the accompanying loss of the French provinces of Alsace and Lorraine to the newly created German state. The war that formed the modern nation state of Germany had toppled the French government and brought humiliation to an entire nation. The 'great revenge' captured the minds of many Frenchmen and the opportunity to regain the lost territory from Germany was of paramount importance.

All of these factors contributed to the outbreak of the First World War; the only thing lacking was a spark to ignite the combustible ingredients and set the continent ablaze. That spark came in June of 1914 with the assassination of Archduke Franz Ferdinand, the heir to the throne of the Austro-Hungarian Empire, by Serbian radicals. The assassination of the Archduke and his wife Sophia, while riding in an open car during a state visit to the city of Sarajevo in the Austrian province of Bosnia-Herzegovina, brought Austrian demands on Serbia which could not, and would not, be met. Pleading innocence, Serbia relied on its large and powerful ally, Russia, to help it resist Austria's ultimatum and threat of war. This in turn induced Austria's ally, Germany, to interpret Russia's actions as an act of war and to simultaneously mobilise its armed forces against Russia's ally, France. According to Germany's prescribed military doctrine, the Schlieffen Plan, an immediate invasion of France was required in order to achieve a rapid victory and avoid defeat. This invasion required a thrust through neutral Belgium, and the ensuing invasion and German occupation of Belgium brought Great Britain into the war. Suddenly, and for no concrete or conceivable reason, Europe was on the brink of a continental war that no one seemed either willing or able to avoid. By the end of the first week of August 1914, all of the major powers, including Germany and Austria-Hungary (to be known as the 'Central Powers') and Great Britain, France and Russia (to be known as the 'Allies') had declared war on each other. Italy had prudently remained on the sideline and refused to honour its original alliance, only to join the war in 1915 on the opposite side, with the Allies.

To its own regret and remorse, Europe had plunged into the abyss of one of the greatest, deadliest and far-reaching events in human history. The world would never be the same.

German General Alfred von Schlieffen who devised the German strategy for a quick two front victory over France and Russia. Schlieffen, who died in 1913, envisioned a great flanking attack through Belgium that would envelop Paris and rapidly defeat France. The possible success of the plan has been debated ever since. (Library of Congress, Bain Collection)

THE SCHLIEFFEN PLAN

The Schlieffen Plan was the intended method of German deployment to confront both Russia and France. This was done by fighting a holding action against the Russians in the east while simultaneously launching a massive 'swinging door' through Belgium into France in the west, and surrounding Paris to enable an early victory. The plan's feasibility is still being debated, however most experts believe it could not have achieved success. In the event of the summer of 1914, the plan failed to bring Germany victory.

3
PRE-SOMME SITUATION

The situation of the First World War in 1916 was one of stalemate. Two huge forces were locked in a ceaseless struggle. The 'Central Powers' of Germany, Austria-Hungary and the Ottoman Empire (Turkey) were holding all of the territory that they had started the war with, plus large areas of occupied France, Belgium and Russia. The 'Allies', consisting of a larger team of powerful nation states (namely France, Russia and Britain), controlled most of the oceans, had superior availability to worldwide trade and transport, and possessed access to the vast mineral, commercial and financial resources of their global colonial empires. Italy, having declined its pre-war obligation to the Central Powers, had decided to join the Allies in May 1915. The Allied partners also included large and wealthy British components such as Australia, New Zealand, Canada and India, as well as numerous colonial detachments from international French possessions. It was a formidable array of global strength.

Most pre-war experts never envisioned Europe being engulfed in a war of this vast dimension. When war arrived in August of 1914 it was widely expected that the war would be short, entail intense but brief fighting, and certainly be over by Christmas. All of these predictions were grossly misplaced. After several weeks of initial movement and invasion by the German forces into France (the failed Schlieffen Plan), the European war had settled into a stalemated condition along three major fronts. By mid-1915 the European armies found themselves in an Italian–Austrian front locked in the mountains of northern Italy; a broad eastern European front between Russia and the combined powers of Germany and Austria-Hungary, where there was still considerable tactical movement; and the tightly stalemated western European front of partially occupied France and Belgium where Anglo-French armies had merged to block and hold back the powerful German army after narrowly preventing the capture of Paris at the war's outset. Large battles had already been fought on all three fronts, although a strategic breakthrough had yet to be achieved. Casualties, however, had erupted into enormous numbers. Equipment and material requirements had quickly been exhausted, and the demand for more troops, food, ammunition and weapons was only growing. Although the Germans had won a major victory early in the war against the Russians at Tannenburg, they were now forced to provide two complete armies to wage war on two vast fronts. The Eastern/Russian front involved containing the numerically superior, though indifferently led and less amply equipped, Russian army. The Western/Anglo-French front had bogged down into a numbing stalemate after the failure of an early German attempt to rapidly take Paris and quickly win the war. All of the armies, particularly on the Western Front, had literally dug-in to avoid the lethal firepower of modern artillery and machine guns. Trench warfare became the rule and the trench lines extended roughly 450 miles across north-western Europe from the North Sea to the Swiss frontier in France.

There were, of course, other important battle fronts: the German use of submarine warfare in the Atlantic to halt vital Allied importation of supplies from around the world, particularly from North America; the blockading of German seaports by the British Royal Navy to likewise prevent the Central Powers from also importing necessary food and resources; and the war in the Middle East as the Allies attempted to knock Turkey out of the war and open a supply route to Russia through the Black Sea, culminating in the disastrous failed attempt at Gallipoli in 1915.

French soldiers in a trench protected by barbed wire. (Library of Congress)

With the war therefore stalemated, various major Allied attacks proceeded on both Eastern and Western Fronts, but all proved insufficient to achieve a breakthrough, although the price paid in casualties and equipment became shockingly larger and larger. Various technologies and inventions were explored, devised and employed to accelerate a breakthrough: aeroplanes, poison gas and eventually tanks, but nothing could pierce the seemingly impenetrable lines of fixed, deeply dug-in defences backed by powerful weaponry and determined manpower. The Germans initiated the first renewed bid with a massive attack at the fortified city of Verdun in north-eastern France. German high command decided to 'bleed' the French army to death by inducing the French to defend Verdun at all costs and thereby die in the process with little, or at least less, cost than to the Germans. However, the battle soon morphed into an all-out German attempt to take Verdun and its surrounding ring of forts. The battle raged for ten months at a cost to France of an estimated 450,000–500,000 casualties, which, as predicted by the German high command, refused to concede the position and vowed to defend it at all costs. The Germans, who foolishly lost sight of their original goal, endured 350,000–400,000 casualties.

Therefore, by the summer of 1916, with France teetering on the brink of defeat at Verdun, and with a hopelessly stalemated Western Front, the British reluctantly agreed to join in a huge and potentially decisive joint Anglo-French attack somewhere along the Western Front. The attack would serve to relieve pressure on the desperate French at Verdun and possibly achieve the dream of breaking through the German lines and winning the war. Accordingly, the French and British high command determined that an attack along the Somme river valley, in a previously quiet sector of the Western Front where the Anglo-French armies were linked, would hold the greatest opportunity for success to achieve both of these strategic goals.

The area of Picardy in north-western France is dominated by farms and the slow-flowing Somme and Ancre rivers. This region was not the first choice of the British high command. The British commanding officer, General Sir Douglas Haig, preferred a renewed attempt further north in the Flanders area of Belgium. Attempting a breakthrough in Flanders was thought by Haig to be better suited for an offensive. This would also help relieve pressure from Germany's threat to the English Channel and North Sea ports, a naval consideration that was always dear to the hearts of Britain's war planners. It would also, if successful, provide an overwhelming tactical advantage and opportunity for rolling up the German front from a powerful northerly angle, potentially enveloping the entire German

Above left: Somme battlefield looking due east toward the town of Albert with the statue of the Golden Madonna atop the Albert church of Notre Dame. Many letters sent home by the soldiers from the Somme battlefield mention this statue. It was across this field and towards the foreground that the British Army repeatedly attacked the German positions at the Battle of the Somme. (Author's collection)

Above right: General Sir Douglas Haig, who sought to bring about General John French's removal, and became commander of the British Army for the remainder of the war. Haig remains one of the most controversial of all British officers. (Author's collection)

north–south position. There was also disagreement as to the suitability of the terrain in the Somme region for successful offensive operations. The British would be attacking over flat, gently rolling plain which sloped uphill. It was known that the German position was well dug-in and reinforced with deep timber and concrete bunkers. Furthermore, it was not known what precisely the British were to do if they did indeed break through – what their immediate tactical objectives would then become, and how seizing those objectives would translate into further penetration. The British were also woefully short of heavy artillery and particularly high-explosive ammunition, along with the required experience to coordinate artillery with massed infantry assaults. Finally, necessary experience and training for their newly formed million-man army of freshly recruited infantry was sorely lacking. British high command desired several more months to prepare for such a mammoth undertaking, with August being the earliest original

German dugouts along the Somme front. These were deeply dug and reinforced, sometimes to depths of 30–40 feet. Notice the steel beams above the entrance. (Library of Congress, Bain Collection)

date. The French, on the other hand, were desperate for immediate relief of their tenuous position at Verdun and urged the British to attack as soon as possible. The French proposed giving assistance to the British attack by contributing a portion of the attacking forces where the trench lines of the two armies merged, and further promised that the French army would fully participate in the attack while employing their considerably superior weight of artillery firepower into the attacking composition. Another factor prompting the Somme location was its relatively undamaged nature. Other sectors of the front had been chewed up by previous combat, making fresh attacks exceedingly difficult due to the wreck of villages and towns, structures and physical terrain. French insistence won out and preparations began for the planned attacks in the Somme.

These decisions were consummated at a conference at Chantilly, France in December 1915 between French commander-in-chief General Joseph Joffre and British General Sir Douglas Haig.[3] As the Verdun situation became more intense and problematic for French survival, the desperation provoked Joffre to continually advance the date that the Somme offensive should commence. As French reinforcements to Verdun were increased, the degree of participation by the French in the Somme offensive had to be reduced. It was not the situation that either Haig or his government favoured, but circumstances compelled cooperation with the French in order to prevent the French predicament at Verdun from becoming a war-ending disaster.

THE BRITISH ARMY

The soldiers of the British Army were composed of three types of units:

1. The veteran regular army that had opened the war and helped stem the initial German invasion and encirclement of Paris, then proceeded to race to the North Sea in order to prevent the Germans from turning the Allies' flank. This action also kept the English Channel ports and sea passages in the hands of the Allies. It was a professional, well-trained army, experienced, disciplined and well equipped, and had been a significant complement to the success of the Allies to block an early German victory. Initially known as the British Expeditionary Force (BEF), it was also relatively small (roughly 80,000, whereas the French and German armies each numbered a million), comprised barely six full-sized infantry divisions and one division of cavalry, and was undermanned due to the commitments of nearly two years of fighting.

2. The Territorial Force or adjunct British Army, consisting of homeland reserves and the volunteer army that was created upon the opening weeks and months of the war to flesh out the regular army. It too was severely undermanned due to two years of attrition. There were roughly fourteen Territorial infantry divisions at the war's start, but they were expected to receive six months training before being engaged, and officially were not legally required to serve overseas. Added to these groups was the initial volunteer movement that raised nearly 750,000 recruits by September 1914 and over a million by January 1915. By the end of 1915, Britain had enlisted well over 2 million soldiers, but by then the volunteer pool was drying up. This next round of volunteer recruitment became known as the 'Second', or 'Kitchener's' army. At the war's outset, there was no conscription in Great Britain. However, this changed in January 1916 when a conscription act was passed that went into effect by March of 1916. This was to be the army that swelled the ranks to over 4 million within seventy divisions, placed Britain on a comparable strength with Germany and France, and eventually finished the war.

3. Finally, the addition of the British Empire's far-flung reach of colonial volunteers and their various soldier armies that were expected to contribute to the Empire's dedication to the international emergency posed by the German threat. These forces were of considerable number and ranged widely in common training, experience and commitment. Coming mainly from countries like Canada, Australia, New Zealand, India and South Africa, they too were stretched to the limit in number from their original contribution. By the war's end, roughly 2.5 million British colonial and empire soldiers participated in the war.

As mentioned, by the start of 1916 the new campaign to raise a fresh army of 1 million soldiers was implemented by Lord Horatio Kitchener and the high command of the British Army. These soldiers would be called upon to volunteer for 'King and Country', to do their patriotic duty and serve the nation. The call to arms was met by enthusiastic response and the numbers swelled to reinforce the thinning and undermanned ranks of the original BEF. Kitchener's army of volunteers was the foundation of the British army that would travel to France and go 'over the top' on 1 July 1916; this 'new' army of one million volunteers would fight the Battle of the Somme for the next six months. This would be the last major volunteer army, as from early 1916 the bulk of the British Army would be a conscripted one.

Above left: Field Marshal Lord Horatio Kitchener, Secretary of State for War 1914–16. It was Kitchener who called for volunteers including the 'pals' volunteer army that suffered so greatly at the Somme. Kitchener was later killed on a mission to Russia when his ship struck a mine and sank. (Library of Congress, Bain Collection)

Above right: French General Joseph Joffre. It was Joffre who insisted on a British attack on the Somme in 1916 in order to relieve pressure at Verdun. (Library of Congress, Bain Collection)

COMMAND

During the First World War, the British Army on the Western Front was led by two commanders. The first was Sir John French, who led the BEF into the war and served as the supreme British commander in the early Western Front battles that helped halt the German invasion into Belgium and France. He later conducted the first and second battle of Ypres and the heavily committed British offensives along the Western Front at Neuve Chapelle and at Loos. All of these battles failed to achieve a breakthrough or make significant tactical gains, and all suffered enormous casualties. There were other problems during Sir John French's command: a lack of high explosive artillery shells, which was out of his control and a problem that would plague the British for the first three years of the war; and General French's inability to get along with the French army's high command. Therefore, in late 1915, French resigned his command

and returned to England as commander of the home forces. He was replaced by Sir Douglas Haig, who would lead the British Army for the duration of the war. It is Douglas Haig who would plan and execute the Battle of the Somme.

Haig was born in Scotland and had been trained as a cavalry commander while serving in various military capacities around the British Empire. He had seen combat service in the South African Boer War and had won high praise as a corps commander during the early stages of the First World War. Haig had served as an advisor and aide-de-camp to King George V, providing him acquaintance with the king that would help promote him, and later retain him, as the war progressed. Haig had played an effective and significant role in the stopping of the German invasion in the summer of 1914, and had further impressed as a field commander during early offensives conducted by Sir John French. It was Haig's avowed and open disappointment at and disapproval of General French's conduct of these attacks – attacks which virtually wiped out the initial BEF – that brought Haig into focus as a potential replacement of French.

Haig's initial goal in 1916 was to achieve a breakthrough, and he felt that the best location for such a breakthrough was in Belgium at the extreme northern end of the Allied front. Attacks along the Belgian Ypres front would provide safety for the British channel ports along the English Channel and hold opportunity for a breakthrough into and around the German lines, across Belgium and into Germany proper. His feeling was that the previous commander, General French, was inadequate for such an undertaking, lacking breadth of strategic and tactical vision, energy and confidence. Haig was confident and convinced that he could persevere and succeed where French had failed. Haig remains one of the most controversial leaders of the First World War, both in method and achievement. Volumes have been written for and against his tactics and strategy, and debate still rages as to his role. Was he a hapless butcher with no imagination? Or, under the circumstances and situation, was he doing the best that anyone could do at that time? Ultimately, the Allies would succeed and Germany would capitulate; but was it because of, or in spite of, Haig and his controversial team of officers and tactics? The question is still debated.

Haig was supported by several other veteran high-ranking commanders who would play an important role in the Somme campaign. Haig chose General Sir Henry Rawlinson to command the British Fourth Army that would conduct the Somme offensive. Rawlinson was one of the few high British commanders whose background was as an infantry commander. To Rawlinson, Haig gave the task of actively planning the details of the Somme assault. Rawlinson's views on tactics basically complied and agreed with those of Haig's, but they did disagree over certain elements of preparation, responsibility and training. Haig of course had the final decision.

Rawlinson proposed a more conservative 'bite and hold' tactic that would seize a frontline German position, consolidating this position by bringing up fresh troops and repositioning the necessary artillery for the next 'bite' of German positions. This would be repeated as the offensive went forward. Haig was more inclined to attempt to penetrate deeply and follow up any successes with aggressively reinforced thrusts to achieve the hoped-for breakthrough. Rawlinson also preferred an extended pre-attack bombardment to destroy German defences, while Haig believed in shorter and more intense bombardments giving the Germans less warning of an impending attack. Haig was determined to reach for the 'big' breakthrough.

Like Haig, many fellow officers were cavalry commanders and remained quite sentimental and optimistic about what a cavalry charge could still accomplish – even in the lethal format of the First World War. In fact, at the Somme Haig insisted

Below left: General Henry Rawlinson, Haig's choice to plan the Somme offensive and lead the British Fourth Army. (Library of Congress, Bain Collection)

Below right: German general and commander-in-chief Eric von Falkenhayn. It was his strategy to 'bleed' France white at Verdun. At the Somme he ordered repeated counter-attacks to challenge every British attack and advance. He was replaced during the Somme campaign. (Library of Congress, Bain Collection)

that four cavalry divisions be ready and poised to reinforce a breakthrough, if one was achieved. In the event, the cavalry never came into play. However, the man chosen to lead this unit was another cavalry-trained officer, Sir Hubert Gough, who was also in charge of the British reserve force at the Somme. Later in the war, Gough would be blamed and sacked for an alleged inability to be properly prepared for the 1918 German offensive that nearly captured Paris and won the war for Germany.

The German high command in 1916 was under the overall command of Erich von Falkenhayn, the general responsible for the 'meat grinder' war being conducted at Verdun, a battle so intense that the French begged the British to relieve pressure on the area by mounting a large assault at the Somme. Falkenhayn believed that the industrial and material strength of the Anglo-French Allies would eventually overwhelm the German Western Front, and he was therefore determined to split the Allies and drive the British out of the war. To do this would require reducing the French forces by committing the numerically formidable French army to a battle not fought for position or tactical goal, but as a method of bleeding them dry. As Falkenhayn had predicted, the French poured everything into the defence of the fortresses surrounding Verdun. Falkenhayn also correctly foresaw that the French would then enlist the British to counter-attack elsewhere on the Western Front in order to relieve pressure on the fighting at Verdun. Falkenhayn believed that a defensive holding policy was the solution to defeating the British attack – challenging every British or French attempt at gaining ground and eventually counter-attacking a weakened adversary, splitting the two armies, and driving the British into the sea. This holding policy would be keyed by strongly developed defensive positions maintained in-depth, and by a rigorous system of reinforcement to challenge any assaults while initiating continuous counter-attacks in order to reclaim lost ground.

Direct command of the German Somme front was carried out by Generals Fritz von Below and Max von Gallwitz, under the overall command of Bavarian Crown Prince Rupprecht, a member of the German nobility who was also an experienced and capable military commander. The generals were seasoned and effective commanders with distinguished backgrounds in both offensive and defensive operations. Both were expert in conducting the tactic of maintaining a position with well-defended and reinforced systems of deeply dug underground bunkers, backed by nearby reserve units that would then immediately counter-attack a temporarily lost position. This constant reinforcing tactic would prevent any besieger from gaining a toehold within the German defensive position. These tactics required well-trained soldiers, committed to aggressive action, and they succeeded amazingly well in preventing any major breakthrough by either the British or French attackers. However, the cost to German troop strength was large, since the counter-attacks were frequently as devastating in casualty losses to the Germans as to the original attacking French and British. This back and forth taking and retaking of positions would go on for months at the Somme, as the Germans only grudgingly gave up ground while exacting an enormous toll upon the Allies in killed and wounded. Unfortunately for the Germans, they were being beaten at their own game, for the Germans were actually less able to sustain losing so many men. The British and French, with greater reserves, were better able to continue to pour in more and more manpower – albeit at great loss, but ultimately to the detrimental consequence of the German army.

This goal of victory through attrition would later become General Haig's argument to the criticism of his tactics, although many accused him of only employing this rebuttal after the fact. More pessimistic, or realistic, were the accounts by many German high-ranking officers, that the Battle of the Somme wiped out the 'flower of the German army', and that it would never again be adequately replaced. General von Below, in spite of Germany's stout defence, was worried that more 'victories' such as the Somme would leave Germany with no army left to fight with. And Generals Hindenburg and Ludendorff, jointly replacing Falkenhayn as supreme German commander midway through the Somme campaign, decided that the German army could not continue such a battle on equal terms, and in early 1917 withdrew to a more defendable position 15 miles to the rear.[4] If either side was declaring victory after the Somme, the British in gaining 8 miles and wearing down the Germans, or the Germans in preventing a breakthrough, it would be a classic description of a Pyrrhic victory.

Indeed, Allied domination in material, food, equipment, manpower and overall ability to reinforce its armies would eventually lead to the breakdown of the German war machine and its defeat and surrender. Whether this was actually the pre-ordained plan envisioned by Allied commanders Haig and Joffre at this point in time remains debatable. Certainly, Haig later claimed this was the entire intention of the Somme campaign: to relieve pressure on Verdun as requested by Joffre and to begin the methodical grinding down of the German army which Haig believed would lead to victory. Much of Haig's 'belief' is strongly contested by many historians who have concluded that his rationale came decidedly after scores of disastrous attacks at the Somme for no territorial or tactical gain. Either way, the German army did successfully defend its position but at a cost nearly equal to that of the Allies – a cost that it could not continue to sustain if it expected to win the war.

Haig had been convinced of the necessity of an early summer offensive by his French counterpart General Joffre, hero of the French victory at the First Battle of the Marne that spared a French defeat at the opening of the war in 1914. Joffre's senior commander of the French northern flank in the Somme sector was General Ferdinand Foch. Foch's French forces were to combine with the British in the attack of the German positions at the Somme. Two of Foch's senior generals of note, and in actual command of the French assaults at the Somme, were Generals Emile Fayolle and Joseph Micheler. In their assaults at the Somme, both generals succeeded in gaining ground at a more economical cost of manpower than the British. The French were also able to quickly achieve more objectives, suffer fewer casualties and secure the extreme southern flank of the Somme sector. However, due to a lack of supporting troops, the French were unable to capitalise on their territorial gains and pursue a successful breakthrough. Fayolle was in his mid-sixties, but had a fine reputation with his soldiers due to his reluctance to waste manpower, instead relying upon superior concentration of weapons and firepower rather than blood. He was a critic of the British attacks at the Somme, and a firm believer in the heavy use of artillery to soften up a position before attacking with infantry, succeeding in short but solidly held gains. Micheler, like British General Gough, would later be relieved of command due to the German breakthrough two years later in the spring of 1918. Fayolle would advance in command and become the commanding general for the entire French centre during the Allied victory campaign in the summer and fall of 1918. Foch would eventually replace Joffre as overall French commander and later become the supreme Allied commander in their final November 1918 victory over the Germans.

For the British, Haig's command is frequently condemned and heavily criticised, although these arguments have see-sawed back and forth over the succeeding decades. Certainly, at the Somme the British bore the brunt of a seemingly fruitless and endless campaign with no obvious positive result. Haig's perceived lack of imagination in the Somme attacks hides the fact that he was open to the use of more aeroplane reconnaissance for observation and the introduction of the new invention, the tank, which was just appearing. In addition, he experimented with the strategy of a 'creeping barrage', This is a method of protecting advancing soldiers by laying down a curtain of continuous artillery shell fire only a few yards in front of the attacking waves of soldiers. It prevents the defenders from engaging their guns and returning fire. As the barrage creeps forward, so do the assaulting attackers. It requires precision artillery delivery, perfect timing and co-ordination by infantry and artillery, and well-trained soldiers of both units.

Above left: French General Ferdinand Foch, army group commander at the Battle of the Somme, later commander-in-chief of all Allied forces. (Library of Congress, Bain Collection)

Above right: Foch became commander-in-chief in 1918, a decision that helped lead the Allies to victory by forming a unified command that previously had been absent in the Allied leadership. (Author's collection)

When properly used it is extremely effective. However, Haig's belief in the use of the creeping barrage was negated by the untrained nature of his new million-man army and the poor coordination between his infantry and the artillery's shell delivery. Later in the war, with experience and dedication, the creeping barrage tactic would be considerably improved upon and by the end of the war the British Army had succeeded in mastering this technique, but at the Somme, the British infantry suffered horrific casualties due to the poor coordination from the accompanying artillery units.

Haig later explained that it was a learning process for him and his commanding lieutenants such as Rawlinson, but for the 500,000 or so British soldiers who became casualties at the Somme it was of little consolation. Also to Haig and Rawlinson go the blame for the complete lack of battlefield communication that plagued the British on the first day of the Somme and continued to affect them throughout the Somme campaign. Attacks were repeatedly ordered in the face of

GUNS

Howitzer
Cannon used to launch projectiles at high trajectory with a steep angle of descent. Usually features a shorter barrel than a 'long' gun or cannon.

Mortar
Very high-trajectory short-range weapon. Can launch a heavy or lightweight shell at a very close distance. Very effective for close-range combat such as trench warfare.

Maxim machine gun
Rapid firing automatic weapon invented by American Hiram Maxim that could spew 500 bullets a minute. Usually operated by a three-man crew and by all sides during First World War.

'French .75'
Revolutionary rapid-firing, breech-loading field gun produced in great quantities by the French.

'Big Bertha' howitzer
Long-range heavy-duty artillery cannon built by the German Krupp ironworks. Powerfully destructive weapon, capable of delivering awesomely explosive power with accuracy at 5–8 miles.

unachievable goals and suicidal conditions for success. The lack of meaningful artillery preparation; the method of crossing the no man's land battlefield, walking in long, slow and vulnerable waves; the over four month length of the campaign in spite of repeated lack of success; all of these failures fall on the shoulders of the commander-in-chief. If indeed Verdun was relieved to the salvation of the French army, and if the gains were beneficial two years later in victory, it certainly came at painful price in manpower and human suffering.

4

PREPARATION

The hope for a breakthrough of German lines at the Somme, to be followed up by an anticipated war-winning deep penetration and victory, had already been discarded due to the enormous pressure and potential disaster of the French position at Verdun. The thunderous German attacks at Verdun were relentless and the French, though determined in their retaliatory counter-attacks, were at the breaking point. Therefore, by the spring of 1916, the goal of the Somme attack had been reduced considerably in both scale and scope. Its main objective now was to relieve the pressure of the German attacks at Verdun; seize the railhead of Bapaume 9 miles behind the German front lines; and possibly, with luck, begin to roll up the German lines north of the River Somme – or at least be in a secure position to threaten to do so.

Planning encompassed an attacking front of 15 to 20 miles, a front that was later reduced. The British would contribute twenty-five divisions of infantry, later lowered to thirteen, and the French another forty, which was later shaved to five attacking divisions of infantry due to continued commitment on the stressed defence at Verdun. What had originally been planned at the December 1915 Chantilly Conference as a monumental war-winning attack, was now being designed to relieve pressure on Verdun and set the stage for further increased attacks at a later date. The French, with veteran soldiers and superior artillery, would attack the southern sector of the Somme region, while the British, with more miles of front to the north but less artillery per mile, would attempt to breach the northern area of the Somme valley. The British would also be introducing their newly expanded but less experienced army to its first major encounter. Lack of sufficient training and experience by both British infantry and artillery forces would handicap their offensive efforts. More pronounced would be a lack of concentrated heavy, high-explosive artillery support that would dramatically prevent the hoped-for elimination of the well-developed German defences. Attacking British forces would be impeded by uncut and intact barbed wire obstacles and German defenders, who quickly emerged from their deep bunkers to man their deadly machine gun positions.

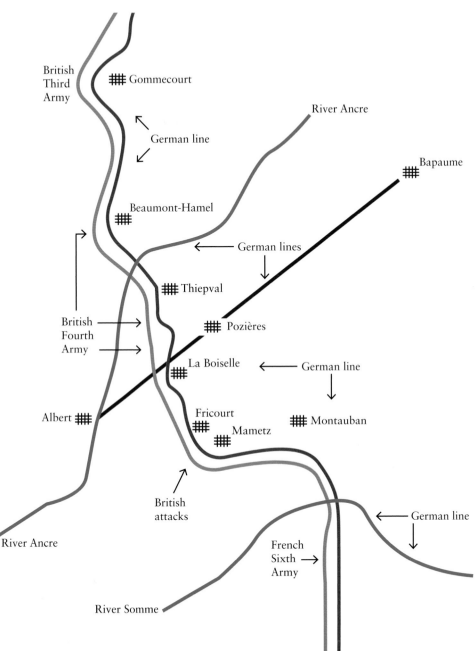

British
Third
Army

Gommecourt

River Ancre

↖ German line ↙

Bapaume ###

Beaumont-Hamel
###

← German lines ↓

↗

Thiepval

British → Fourth Army →

Pozières

La Boiselle
###

← German line ↓

Albert ###

Fricourt
###
Mametz
###

Montauban

↗ British attacks

River Ancre

← German line ↓

French Sixth → Army

River Somme

Map of the Somme sector of north-western France and designated for the July 1916 offensive. Green depicts the Ancre and Somme Rivers, red the German front line and blue the British and French front lines. The town of Bapaume was the overall British objective, a distance of less than 15 miles from the starting front lines. The towns of Mametz, Fricourt, La Boiselle, Montauban, Thiepval, and Beaumont Hamel were all designated for conquest on 'Day One' but most would require four months of hard fighting to gain. Bapaume was never reached.

British Commander Douglas Haig met with his chief planner, Fourth Army Commander Lieutenant-General Henry Rawlinson, and decided that a diversionary attack to the north, at the German strongpoint of Gommecourt, using Lieutenant-General Henry Allenby's Third Army, would serve as a useful compliment to the offensive. Allenby was opposed to this plan, fearing his flank would be unprotected and his army in danger of intense enfilade exposure. Such proved to be true and the Third Army suffered extensive casualties for little or no purpose. To the south, where the French Sixth Army merged with the British Fourth Army, the French would conduct attacks against the German positions near the town of Montauban. Rawlinson's plan envisioned the concentrated use of heavy artillery over the course of a prolonged saturation bombardment lasting a week. This sustained barrage would hopefully achieve three goals: effectively eliminate the German barbed wire in front of the German positions; devastate and destroy the German frontline trenches including their fortified machine gun nests; and reduce or disable the German ability to reinforce their collapsed front. The deep shelling of the connecting trenches behind the German forward front line trench system would prevent the Germans from mounting their own counter-attacks. Upon seizing and securing the first line of German trenches, the British 'big' guns would be moved forward and the process would be repeated until the second

German soldiers using the Maxim machine gun. This water-cooled weapon which could dominate a large section of battlefield was employed by all armies during the First World War. (National Archives)

line of German trenches could be stormed and taken. This was the 'bite and hold' tactic that Rawlinson favoured. Eventually, with success, the attack would pierce the German lines and a possible breakthrough could be developed. This was the hoped-for breakthrough that Haig sought. If nothing else, the Germans would be forced to commit to a sustained defence and thus relieve the desperate situation on the French defenders at Verdun. The Bapaume railhead would be acquired, and the potential for the roll up of the German lines to the north would be established. Such was the overall goal for the Somme attack.

The assault was to be waged over a front of 15 miles, however the main British thrust would be conducted over a 10-mile section between the French position at Montauban in the south and extending to the River Ancre in the north, where the British Third and Fourth Armies met. Nine British divisions would spearhead the assault along this 10-mile stretch of German line, with an additional three divisions holding a 3-mile position on the northerly left flank. The French would secure the southern flank and attempt to seize territory within its own sector. Behind the British lines would be four reserve divisions, ready to expand and complete the breakthrough if obtained. Among the Day One objectives for the British offensive were the German-held fortified French towns and villages of Serre, Beaumont-Hamel, Thiepval, Pozières, La Boisselle, Fricourt and Mametz.

German 210 mm howitzer produced in large numbers by the Krupp Armaments Company in Germany. A powerful and effective weapon. (Author's collection)

To initially destroy the German positions, a massive 1,500 gun artillery barrage would be conducted for at least five days in advance of the attack, with a ratio of one gun for every seventeen yards of German front. Combined, these guns were to launch 1.5 million shells onto the German position during the week leading up to the attack. These guns would be comprised of numerous calibres, including very 'heavy' (9.2 inches or larger) long guns, howitzers, field guns and mortars. The barrage would be conducted around the clock for a week, but the heaviest concentration would be fired every morning from 6:30 to 7:45. A constant, but reduced, barrage would continue throughout the day and night. One half of the guns would rest at night while the other half maintained a steady bombardment.

SHRAPNEL

Bits of metal from an exploding shell that are lethally dispersed in all directions, mainly as an anti-personnel weapon. Shrapnel is named after Henry Shrapnel, a British Army officer who developed an exploding shell. Artillery shells and hand grenades both feature shrapnel.

Two types of artillery ammunition would be used in the barrage: shrapnel and high-explosive. Shrapnel is mainly a personnel-killing shell employing a fearsome array of small and deadly splintering metal objects that burst into numerous bits of lethal metal – such as in a shot gun shell – and pre-set to explode at various predetermined heights. Raining a deadly and horrific blizzard of metallic pellets over a victimized area, it is merciless in its lethality, inflicting murderous devastation upon anything within its radius of effect. Artillery is also effective in destroying barbed wire, a key element in the planned preparation for the assault on the German lines. As he approaches enemy lines, being snarled and entangled in a huge spool of barbed wire while exposed to enemy fire is the last thing an attacking soldier wants to be forced to engage or contend with.

TRENCH WARFARE

Trench warfare was the name given to the style of fighting which stalemated the two opposing armies across Europe during the First World War. Each side dug extensive ditches and underground bunkers for protection from the continuous artillery and machine-gun fire. No man's land was the area between the opposing trenches, usually littered with debris, shell holes and barbed wire, that had to be crossed on any offensive attack. Barbed wire, originally designed for use on farms to keep animals in separate pastures, was also effective at delaying charging soldiers. Placed in front of trenches to trap the advancing men, this is an example of a peaceful invention converted into a wartime tool.

Shrapnel, however, is ineffective at destroying barbed wire, especially when the detonation of the shell is poorly timed. Nor is shrapnel effective at demolishing deep dugouts of concrete and timber. If the shell bursts too high, it scatters the lethal bits of metal and loses its potency. If too low, it ploughs into the muddy sod where its impact and damage capability is eliminated. British soldiers attacking the German front lines on the first day of the Battle of the Somme were instructed and trained with the expectation that the barbed wire would be removed and destroyed by the pre-attack artillery barrage before they ever approached the German line. Tragically, for a variety of reasons, this turned out not to be the case – and the attack suffered dramatically for it. Further reducing the shrapnel's effectiveness was the fact that fuses on the shrapnel shells either did not function properly or were poorly timed by inexperienced gunners, resulting in the shrapnel shells doing little or no damage.[5] Two-thirds of the 1.5 million shells launched before the attack were of the shrapnel variety.[6] This bombardment would supposedly guarantee the expectant result of killing would-be defenders while also removing the deadly barbed wire from in front of the German positions. Instead, the attacking British infantry frequently discovered a full array of healthy barbed wire awaiting their arrival in front of the German trenches and defending Germans emerging from their deeply dug bunkers manning machine guns.

Of the other one-third of the shells, less than 10 per cent were of the high-explosive variety. This type of artillery shell was intended to destroy the steel and timber reinforced German bunkers that formed an underground labyrinth of protection for the German soldiers burrowed deep under their front lines. After enduring the devastating and punishing artillery barrage, these defenders, assuming they survived with their wits still about them, would then race to their trench parapets and machine gun nests, to greet the arrival of the British infantry assault. Surviving German defenders would be able to man machine guns to successfully mow down the attacking British assaulters, which

Above: British soldiers firing a long-range cannon near the front. These guns featured a low trajectory and fired great distances, howitzers fired a higher trajectory to target nearer positions. (Library of Congress, Bain Collection)

Below: British 8-inch howitzers of the 39th Siege Battery in action along the Fricourt-Mametz valley in August 1916 during the Battle of the Somme. (Library of Congress)

they indeed proceeded to do in ferocious fashion. Unfortunately for the British artillery – and their infantry attack units – high-explosive shells were in short supply, and the British were woefully lacking in the number of large 'big guns' that could penetrate the deeply reinforced underground German bunkers. The British only possessed thirty-four pieces of heavy artillery of 9.2 inches or larger.[7] The French, with a much smaller front to attack on the Somme, possessed double the amount of 'big guns' to pulverise the German positions before commencing their attack. The success of the French assaults on Day One of the Somme can largely be attributed to their superior 'big gun' firepower. The French engaged a greater ratio of 'big guns' per mile of front and were capable of inflicting a greater concentration of accurate fire to enable their attacking soldiers a far better opportunity to seize their assigned positions.

For the early part of the war the French were superior to the British at effectively using massed artillery of larger calibre and with far greater use of high explosive. The French were also better at the production of more big guns and providing the necessary high-explosive capacity for the blasting of enemy defences in front of an infantry charge. It may also have contributed to a naive overconfidence of their ability to successfully attack and penetrate the German lines. In 1917, the French offensives under General Robert Nivelle proved to be of such massive slaughter and futility that the French army temporarily mutinied and refused to attack again under the Nivelle command.

To further enhance the initial attack, the British had excavated a group of tunnels that reached beneath the German trenches. Nineteen of these mineshaft-style tunnels had been completed by 1 July and the start of the battle. The tunnels were packed with explosives and were detonated shortly before the attack began. Intelligence reconnaissance had identified some of the strongest German positions, which were designated for these great mines that held tons of high explosive. The huge Lochnagar crater at La Boiselle remains clearly visible to this day.

Above: The Maxim .50-calibre water-cooled machine gun, invented by American Hiram Maxim and shown here with American soldiers, could spit out over 500 bullets a minute. (Library of Congress, Bain Collection)

Below: A trench mortar here being loaded by American soldiers later in the war. Mortars were capable of a very high trajectory in order to shell a very close position, such as across the short distance of no man's land. (US Army Signal Corps, Library of Congress)

Most of the 'Day One' craters detonated by the British Army have been filled in and farmed over. The huge Lochnagar Crater remains as a monument to the horrific devastation that took place on the first day of the Battle of the Somme. The crater's rim measures over 140 metres. (Author's collection)

THE GERMAN LINE

The need for high-explosive shells was known to the British high command in advance of the Somme battle. Deep underground German bunkers had earlier been captured and inspected by the British along the Somme sector.[8] The findings concluded that not only were these bunkers numerous and deep, sometimes to a depth of thirty feet, but also extremely well designed and virtually impervious to damage unless met with a direct hit of high-explosive shells. The chalky earth along the Somme front was conducive to the construction of dugouts which, when combined with steel or timber reinforcement, could survive all but the heaviest barrage of the biggest guns.

Further difficulties in the Somme sector were posed by the gently rolling open farm fields featuring divided ridge lines broken by small villages and wooded hills; these were perfect locations for a defender to employ as strong flanking positions and were inherently resistant to frontal attacks. The second line German trenches were frequently on opposite sides of a ridge from the first line trench and perhaps

Above: British 18-pound gun. (Courtesy of Jonathan Reeve)

Below: German 7.7 cm field gun similar to the French .75. (Author's collection)

a mile to the rear. An attacking unit that successfully overcame the first German line would have to start all over in order to take the second line of defence. This would involve fully securing the first position and warding off any counter-attacks, surviving pinpoint counter artillery fire from the German guns (which were virtually unobservable by British ground reconnaissance), and moving the British 'big guns' to a new forward position in order to both impede the German artillery and to begin the process of reducing the next line of trenches. All these situations created a formidably daunting prescription for success under the best of conditions and fortune.

BRITISH INFANTRYMEN – THE 'TOMMIES'

Each attacking British infantryman was trained to expect a depleted or weakened German front line. He believed he would be able to quickly and easily secure the designated targets, and was prepared and equipped to push on and engage the next line of defence. Therefore, each soldier was to carry roughly 65–70 pounds of pack, walk upright at a reasonable pace, and be laden with enough ammunition, food and gear to establish a stronghold on the conquered line. Reinforcements would soon follow, and another 'bite' of the German defence would be inaugurated. The reserve divisions, including cavalry, would be deployed in the area of breakthrough as determined by observers ascertaining the tactical situation. The artillery would be moved forward and the next stage of attack would commence.

TOMMY

British soldiers in the trenches during the war were nicknamed 'Tommies'. It is said that the name 'Tommy Atkins' was the example name on conscription sheets.

Nicknamed 'Tommies', the British soldier in the initial lead waves of attack would typically wear a steel helmet, carry his rifle and bayonet, two gas helmets, 220 rounds of ammunition, two Mills bombs (hand grenades), two empty sandbags, a spade, wire-cutters, a flare and also his personal gear plus tins of food and a water canteen. He was then instructed to cross no man's land at a parade walk and not to sprint until within 20 yards of the enemy position. Following waves were also required to carry stakes for the laying of new barbed

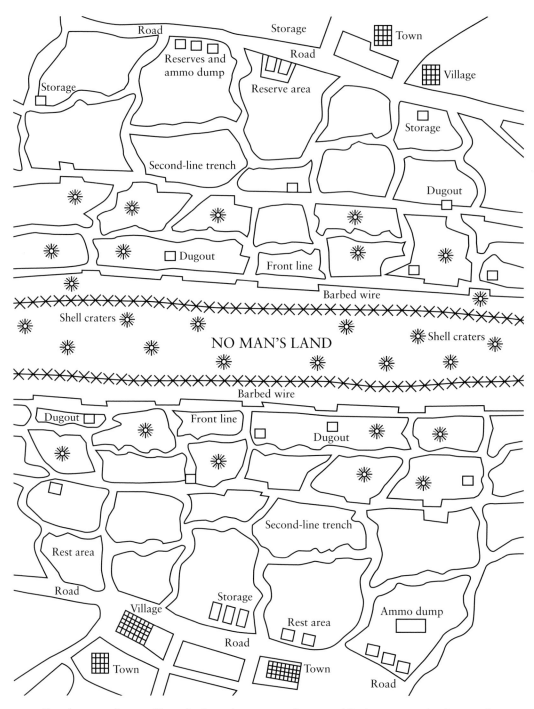

Trench system diagram. 'Front line' trenches connected to second line/reserve trenches in case of retreat, and eventually winding back towards main artery roads, villages, and towns. Connecting trenches provided access to the front lines for rations, water, reinforcement, and equipment.

wire, duckboards and other equipment meant to better secure the captured positions.

Optimism abounded in the British ranks as to the condition of the German trenches prior to the attack. The attacking infantry were to advance in long waves, followed in one minute intervals by another advancing wave, and to expect barbed wire to be removed, trenches demolished and German defenders dead or dazed. Officers were confident that the week-long barrage would provide a safe journey across no man's land, and had conducted training for such a reality. Certainly the unrelenting bombardment of the German lines by the British artillery must have been an agonising ordeal for the Germans to endure. Many Germans were killed and many dugouts, bunkers and pillboxes were destroyed; but nevertheless, many German defenders *did* survive in their rabbit warren of reinforced bunkers, and were able to emerge intact, if numb, and operate their machine guns to lethal effect. Barbed wire had not been cut to the predicted degree and many British soldiers became caught and left exposed to German machine guns. German artillery had not been neutralised and soon zeroed in on the attacking British infantry coming across no man's land. Attacking infantry were swept away by German counter artillery fire within minutes of the cessation of the British barrage. British communication with back line commanders that had been so rigorously prepared and practiced soon disintegrated, and a situation of chaotic futility quickly enveloped the surviving attacking forces. Nearly 60,000 British soldiers would become casualties on the first day of the Somme – one-third of those fatal, and most within the first hour of the attack.

5

SUPPLIES AND TRANSPORT

By May of 1916 the date of the Somme offensive had been agreed upon by Generals Joffre and Haig. Haig had already moved his date to mid-August, but Joffre was adamant that the date could be no later than 1 July or 'the French army would no longer exist', due to the escalating French casualties at Verdun. With over 90,000 casualties sustained through March and climbing to near 200,000 by the end of May, the French were desperate for relief. Preparations for the Somme offensive had already been underway throughout the spring of 1916, and now an increased intensity of training of soldiers, stockpiling of resources, and the means to connect the two were being fully developed. At the same time, the Germans were keenly observing the build-up and knew that a summer offensive of great magnitude could be expected.

Technological innovations of the First World War can be sorted into two categories: those meant to better directly kill the opponent, and those meant to provide the resources and support for the means to kill the opponent. Guns, big or little, need shells and powder. Soldiers, fighting or not, have to be healthy, fed, clothed and watered. Supplying these quantifiable entities requires logistical transport and the First World War necessitated the greatest quantity of supply and resource as yet seen in any war, or in any human endeavour to that point in time. This in turn required the transport of colossal quantities of goods from source to point of consumption. An offensive of the scope and duration conducted at the Somme illuminates this fact.

The size of the armies and the demands in material are staggering. During the Somme campaign of 1916, Great Britain was supporting roughly 1.5 million soldiers, building toward the 2-million-man army that Lord Kitchener felt would eventually be necessary to wage and win an all-out war against Germany. This figure would be reached by the end of 1916 and then maintained until the armistice of 1918. France and Germany had similarly sized armies on the Western Front, with Germany benefiting from shorter interior lines of defence.

The Krupp ironworks in Essen, Germany, famous for its production of high quality weaponry. (Author's collection)

Equipment and provisions were then demanded every day in order to provide for these 'cities of soldiers'. For example, the needs of building just one mile of trench included 900 miles of barbed wire; 6 million sandbags; 1 million cubic feet of timber; and 369,000 feet of corrugated iron. In 1916, the British Army was providing its soldiers with 2,925 cubic feet of tobacco (about one-third larger than the size of an average 20-foot international shipping container) and 70,000 Mills bombs daily.[9] Million-man armies, whether or not in combat, required tons of meat, fruits, vegetables, water and the fuel and hardware to cook, serve and eat it. That consumption required adequate means and methods to dispose of the trash and sewage waste. To provide this mountain of material to these soldiers stationed in the trenches of western Europe, or along the chain of supply, required factories and warehouses in England to produce the material, ships to haul it across the English channel, and extensive railroad lines exclusively designed to transport it to within a reasonable distance of the front. Vehicles, whether animal carts or mechanised trucks, then required roads (in constant need of repair) to transport their burdens to the fighting soldier on the front lines. It was a prodigious operation of enormously detailed logistical planning – and, it had to be maintained and resupplied continuously.

When Verdun was threatened by the Germans in early 1916, and impending defeat was imminent, the newly appointed French commander General Phillipe

British soldiers loading a mammoth siege cannon. (Author's collection)

Petain insisted as the first priority the revamping of the transport system. The 'Voie Sacree' (sacred way) became immortalised in French history as the lifeblood of the French defence of Verdun. Motorised truck transport along a dedicated route operated round-the-clock, in sync and unimpeded, in order to supply and reinforce the embattled Verdun defences with fresh equipment, ammunition and soldiers. It was the first and foremost order of business if Verdun was to be saved and disaster averted.

As the transmission of men and material came closer to the front, the problems and dangers became more pronounced and difficult. Weather, enemy shellfire and the sheer physical demands all combined to make the logistical support of a million-man army not just the key to victory, but necessary for day-to-day survival. Recognising the greater strength and dependability of mechanised vehicles, the French introduced motorised transport early in the war and eventually employed 25,000 trucks during the course of the conflict. Upon entering the war in early 1917, the United States produced 118,000 all-purpose trucks able to carry 3–5 ton loads while negotiating rutted roads and traversing minor obstacles. Of these, over 51,000 would be sent to France. The fundamental means for the delivery of men and goods was by rail, and hundreds of miles of light railways were constructed on both sides of the Western Front between 1914 and 1918. Before 1914, the entire German strategy was based on railroad timetables and the

Above: Typical of the huge siege cannon used in First World War. This is a massive German cannon being completed at the German Krupp Armaments factory in Essen, Germany. Artillery accounted for the majority of wounds and deaths on First World War battlefields. (Library of Congress, Bain Collection)

Below: British large calibre 18 inch (457 mm), rail-mounted howitzer. It could fire a 2,500 lb projectile over 12 miles. On display today at the Royal Armoury. (Author's collection)

Kaiser Wilhelm II reviewing German troops early in the First World War. (Library of Congress, Bain Collection)

ability to move the army efficiently and rapidly to mobilisation sites. Germany's controversial pre-war Schlieffen Plan to defeat France in the first month of the war hinged on this capability. When the Kaiser had second thoughts in 1914 about going to war, he supposedly was told by his commander-in-chief Helmuth von Moltke that the timetable of trains and mobilisation had already been set into motion and now 'it was too late, that the trains had already been loaded and had left'. Such was the dependence and dominance of the railway.

But modern motorised road and rail transport was not nearly enough. Animals were the predominant source of power for the equipment and supplies moved to the front. Not infrequently, manpower shouldered the burden the final few hundred yards as the combatants neared the front line trenches. Over 8 million pack horses were estimated to have been used during the First World War. Most were mistreated as much or more than the soldiers. Hard work was coupled with gruesome wounds and hideous deaths. Most of those 8 million animals did not survive the war, either dying from exertion or killed during exposure to combat. Those that did survive were often worn out, ill, or injured and unable to return to their respective nations. Sadly, many were destroyed or sold to local slaughterhouses. Other animals too were used: dogs as runners and messengers and for carrying packets of medicine, pigeons for carrying messages and information, and mules as beasts of burden.

The killing of horses near the front by gunfire was prolific since the proximity of their activity exposed the pack animals to constant vulnerability. Teams of horses pulled carts, wagons and cannon. Their task was not only demanding, but also essential; without the tens of thousands of draft animals, the day-to-day existence of the fighting soldier would have been impossible. Unfortunately for the poor creatures, the same dangers experienced by the soldiers – overwork, disease and gunfire – extracted a terrible toll on their numbers.

Horses and mules also required hay, fodder and maintenance. Unlike a truck, the horse had to be fed whether in use or not, rain or shine. By weight, a pack horse generally needed ten times the food of a man, and supplying the tens of thousands of animals was one of the largest demands on the armies at the front. Cannon need shells, but heavy cannon required teams of horses to move those cannon into position before they could fire those shells. Teams of horses then brought the countless shells forward that would be fired during the bombardments. For the Somme offensive, the British stockpiled nearly 3 million rounds of artillery ammunition in preparation for the opening of the battle alone. 7,000 miles of telephone cables were laid and 120 new miles of pipe were laid in order to provide fresh water.[10] There were veterinary hospitals for the treatment of sick and wounded animals, and the importance of the animals for the war effort cannot be either ignored or underestimated. Nor can its tragic consequences. The Germans had grossly underestimated both the amount of animal feed required for their war effort, and the length of the war. Running short of fodder, they resorted to mixing sawdust into their animal feed in order to sate the appetites of their draft animals. Unfortunately, it also reduced their work capacity, health and lifespan.

There are numerous accounts of soldiers, under the cover of darkness, liberating otherwise doomed horses trapped in the endless mud of the Western Front. Rescuing horses stuck in mud-holes up to their shoulders and unable to free themselves, soldiers risked their own lives to save not only their beloved animals, but their main means to haul the essentials back and forth to the trench lines. The poignant memorials to these animals throughout France and England are testament to not only their work and importance, but also to the love and devotion felt by their fellow soldiers. One of the best known memorials to the animals is the monument in the town of Chipilly, France. It is dedicated to the British soldiers' love and grief for their painfully suffering horse.

Everything about the First World War was on an immense scale, and materials and transportation were no exceptions. From the quantities of material demanded, to the means and methods to provide these functional requirements, this titanic struggle required logistics of mammoth proportions.

Above: Dead horses and soldiers in 1914. Animals frequently suffered in as great of number as did men. It is estimated that 8 million horses were killed in the First World War. (Library of Congress, Bain Collection)

Below: British soldiers' monument to their beloved and essential horses at Chipilly, France. Horses were not only vital to the transport of supplies but also shared in the soldiers' daily life and death. This memorial was erected by the 58th London Division in gratitude to their horses. (Library of Congress)

6

1 JULY 1916: THE FIRST DAY

Scores of books and articles have been written about the first day on the Somme, probably the best and most frequently cited being Martin Middlebrook's *The First Day On the Somme*. Whether one stands as a critic or a defender of General Douglas Haig's overall strategy in the defeat of Germany, it cannot be denied that the first day on the Somme, indeed, the first hour or even perhaps the first twenty minutes, witnessed one of the greatest slaughters in military history. At 7.30 a.m. on 1 July, 66,000 heavily loaded infantrymen of the British Army climbed 'over the top' and out of their trenches to attack the German front line. They proceeded across no man's land in long waves at a walking pace to encounter firmly entrenched and resolute German defenders. The result was a horror of unparalleled proportions. Over half of the initial attackers would fall as immediate casualties in the opening minutes. The day saw almost 60,000 British casualties, nearly 20,000 of them fatal. Some were gunned down as they left their own trenches; many were riddled with bullets while hung up on the wire in front of the German positions, some while funnelling through the openings of their own wire only a few feet in advance of their own position. Soon, the unsilenced German artillery began to pound the no man's land area, filling the air with lethal shrapnel and annihilating any and all who risked standing or walking across the deadly zone. German soldiers reported their disbelief at the pace of the assaulting British, wave after wave appearing out of the distance as sitting ducks. When the British connecting trenches became clogged with dead and wounded, several officers ordered their men to climb out of second line trenches and cross open field between their own second and first line positions. Many Tommies never even made it to their own first line trench position before being cut to shreds by German machine-gun fire. And still the attacks continued throughout the day.

Communication from the battlefield to the British command headquarters in any meaningful detail or description was prevented by the destruction of telephone lines compliments of the German counter artillery barrage that now

WHAT'S IN AN ARMY?

Although in the First World War unit size often varied, and had to be flexible to meet circumstances, this is the rough size of the army units and their usual commanding rank.

Company	250 men	captain
Battalion	1,000 men	lieutenant-colonel or major
Regiment	2,000 men	colonel
Brigade	4,000 men	brigadier-general
Division	12,000 men	major-general
Corps	50,000 men	lieutenant-general
Army	200,000 men	general

Above: Caribou Monument, emblem of the Royal Newfoundland Regiment, at Beaumont-Hamel. This Canadian maintained area is one of the best preserved sections of the Somme battlefield. Near this location the 1st Newfoundland Regiment went 'over the top' and suffered the loss of more men killed, wounded and missing – 710 including *all* of her officers – than any other battalion on 1 July. (Author's collection)

Opposite above: British soldiers in the trenches getting ready to go 'over the top' at the Somme in July 1916. (Courtesy of Jonathan Reeve)

Opposite below: French soldiers preparing to go 'over the top' and into no man's land. (Library of Congress)

covered the British back line trench positions. British commanders incorrectly assumed that the attacks were going smoothly and successfully, and they ordered up fresh units to capitalise on the imagined gains of the early assaults. These renewed attacks met the same fate as the earlier ones – obliteration. Where reports of advances were known to be stalled, renewed and repeated assaults were ordered forward to reinforce the illusory gains of the surrounding units. This continued on for days, and with the same tragic result.

The litany of stories rapidly attains an identical repetition of result. At Beaumont-Hamel, the Newfoundland Battalion suffered a 90 per cent loss of its combatants. Out of 752 soldiers, the unit lost 684, many falling when ordered to cross above ground from their own second line to their own first line, due to the connecting trenches being hopelessly clogged with dead and wounded. Scores were slain before ever reaching no man's land. The 103rd Tyneside Irish Brigade was forced to go above ground from their own rear lines a full mile behind their own lines. One

The remains of existing trenches in the Canadian sector of the Somme at Beaumont-Hamel showing their depth after a century of weathering. (Author's collection)

battalion lost 600 and another lost 500, each battalion consisting of roughly 1,000 soldiers.[11] The noted military historian John Keegan commented upon their advance: 'Militarily the advance had achieved nothing, and most of the bodies lay on British territory.'[12] By noon the British had committed nearly 100,000 soldiers from 129 battalions to the attack, and casualties had already topped 50,000. Positions that were initially taken were soon retaken in German counter-attacks; other captured areas were isolated and denied reinforcing units due to poor communications, while other units became stranded and forced to retreat from areas only to turn back across the bloodied battlefield that they had fought so hard to secure.

More attacks were ordered up in the afternoon and some progress in the taking of the planned objectives was achieved. Most success came in the southern area of the Somme sector where the British were linked to the supporting French. The French had successfully achieved their goals but lacked any kind of reinforcement to pursue their gains. Some British units in the southern sector were able to seize their objectives by taking advantage of the successful French achievements on their right flank, reaping the benefits of the superior French artillery. But further north on the broader British front, the situation was quite different in both success and casualties.

Here we see a typical bunch of Tommies under fire and going 'over the top'. (Courtesy of Jonathan Reeve)

Up and down the British front the result and reaction was the same. A private in the 11th Suffolk Regiment commented, 'I could see them dropping one after another as the guns swept them. Another minute or so and another came forward … this lot did not get so far as the others.'[13] Another private, from the Seaforth Highlanders, recalled the problem of the uncut barbed wire, and remarked, 'I could see that our leading waves had got caught by their kilts, they were killed hanging on the wire, riddled with bullets.'[14]

A German infantryman, Karl Blenk, later related that during the initial attack, as he and his counterpart defenders peered across the field of no man's land, they 'were surprised to see them walking, we had never seen that before. I could see them everywhere; there were hundreds. The officers were in front. I noticed one of them walking calmly, carrying a walking stick. When we started firing, we just had to load and reload. They went down in their hundreds. You didn't have to aim, we just fired into them'.[15]

As further testimony to the extent of annihilation to some units, the 2nd Battalion of the West Yorkshire Regiment withstood a 70 per cent casualty rate, and the 2nd Battalion of the Middlesex Regiment suffered an even greater 90 per cent rate of casualties. To further increase the tragedy of these losses, many were

Germans stringing barbed wire in front of trenches. (Library of Congress, Bain Collection)

of the 'pals' units that enlisted as members of clubs, shops, factories and town communities. In one bitter day's fighting, many entire elements of young men, chums from an individual town or shop, would be wiped out. Many of these soldiers never fired a shot, never saw an enemy German and never moved beyond their own trench line.

Field Artillery commander R. G. A. Hamilton gives a vivid account of the British trenches, as confused and wounded soldiers clogged the passageways with dead and dying.

> The trench had been blown to pieces in many places and one had to climb out and run across the mounds of thrown-up dirt. In many places the men who had been killed a week or ten days ago were lying in the bottom of the trench, and one had to walk and crawl over them. Many had been half buried by the shells, and only their face or hands or feet could be seen. Many of the bodies were not complete ... To add to the horror of it all, there were millions and millions of flies everywhere ... I was nearly sick with the stench and the sights.[16]

As the first day on the Somme drew to a close, there had been some isolated successes, including some advances of up to a mile on the southern extremity of the sector. The French had achieved nearly all of their objectives, capturing the now destroyed village of Mountaban and seizing 4,000 German prisoners, but were unable to pursue their gains in depth. The French had succeeded because the German sector in front of the French was held by fewer and weaker units; the French had a narrower front and superior artillery preparation, not only in the number of guns per square mile, but also in the better use of high explosives to reduce the German defences before the attack; and previous experience had taught the French to use veteran, special infiltration groups ahead of the heavier main attack in order to weaken German strong spots and better prepare the emphasised chosen assault zone. Additionally, the French faced terrain which was more suitable for attacking. Unlike the central British sector, which was mainly rolling and gently uphill, the French sector offered friendlier geography, and French field commanders were encouraged to not take reckless chances, but instead to secure that which could be obtained at a reasonable cost. Even so, there was no hope for a break out, and no real accomplishment in terms of military or tactical objectives.

The British succeeded in their stated goals of capturing the villages of Fricourt and Mametz that jutted out in a salient, and provided the British artillery with a dominant three-sided artillery barrage that was successfully engaged. Even so, infantry casualties were heavy in those successful operations. In some instances, such as the temporary capture of the Schwaben Redoubt, a highly sought British objective, the conquest could not be maintained due to the lack of British reinforcements. Because of the lack of communication and the aggressive German counter attacks, the hard-won position, gained at such great human cost, was forfeited. It would take another three months of bitter, hard fighting and innumerable more deaths to finally retake the position.

Nowhere had a German second line trench been penetrated and few tactical gains had actually been achieved. Little, if any, operational advantage was accomplished other than the two previously mentioned fortified villages being captured with a narrow overall gain of only a mile in a front covering a total of over 23 miles. This modest gain came at the cost of some 60,000 casualties in a single day, with nearly 20,000 of those resulting in death. German casualties were estimated at slightly over 8,000, with perhaps half of those as prisoners. Further complicating the disaster was the complete misunderstanding of the day's result by the British high command. Meaningful communication was virtually non-existent, figures and results were worse than inadequate since many were inaccurate to the

Restored trenches at the battlefield of Vimy Ridge in north-western France as they may have appeared during the First World War. (Author's collection)

point of being drastically overly optimistic. Haig in his journal wrote of the first day that it was a day of 'ups and downs', and that the men were in 'wonderful good spirits', as he and his subordinate Rawlinson failed completely to grasp the extent of the debacle that was unfolding around them. High command deemed the only remedy to any shortcomings of the day was to continue the attacks – which they did, until November 1916. Indeed, the official reports to the London newspaper press reflected this lack of accurate, complete, or correct recognition of the day's lack of success. The *Daily Express* on 3 July claimed the capture of 9,500 prisoners and many villages, including Serre and Contalmaison, neither of which was taken. One correspondent reported, 'everything going well, our troops have carried out their missions. All counter-attacks have been repulsed ... losses have been very slight.'[17] The last is the most telling, as the casualty count alone, above and beyond failing any tactical achievement, would have underscored how any first day accomplishments would have come at a very high price. Gradually, the British government and public would come to learn of the slaughter taking place so near to them, and they would recoil with horror from the knowledge.

To this day, 1 July 1916 has a bitterly tragic significance: incomparable slaughter for no logical or meaningful purpose.

7

THE NEXT FOUR MONTHS

Throughout the month of July, the British continued their attacks along the Somme front. General Joffre was convinced that any let-up in the British attacks would spell doom for the beleaguered French forces defending Verdun. Joffre was acutely aware of the fragility of the Verdun situation and pressed Haig repeatedly and doggedly that the attacks must continue, even against the formidable German defences along Thiepval Ridge. Haig began reconsidering the need to attack this dominant central position of the Somme front, preferring instead to work the flanks where some gradual progress had been made. To this Joffre was furious, insisting that any reduction in the intensity of the assaults would result in collapse at Verdun. Haig firmly reminded Joffre that he, and not Joffre, was in charge of the British Army and its degree of commitment.[18] For the Germans the orders remained the same: hold all territory and at all costs. This German strategy, similar to the French defence at Verdun, was going to make the British pay a heavy price in blood, but by the same token, the Germans were going to also be billed a heavy toll as they ceaselessly counter-attacked every British thrust. German General Fritz von Below, following General Falkenhayn's overall edict, insisted that any lost area must, 'be attacked and wrested back from the enemy'.[19] This of course meant that the Germans were now locked in a struggle that would be as violently lethal to them as it was to the British.

The French continued to make steady but minor gains on the south end of the Somme sector, but lacked any means of following up their profit due to their complete lack of reserves. The capture of seventy German artillery pieces and over 12,000 German prisoners, along with the French army's advance of several miles, inspired renewed hope for the Allied dream of a breakthrough. During the second week of July, the British too had made some progress in the southern sector, as several key villages and strong-points were overrun and captured. For his part, Joffre was upset that Haig was not pushing harder on the northern extreme of the front, but German defences remained stout and British

Thiepval Memorial in the centre of the Somme battlefield. The village of Thiepval was a British objective on 1 July, the first day of the battle, but was not captured until August. (Author's collection)

casualties high in the face of stubborn resistance. General Falkenhayn's demand of continued resistance required increased investment of reserves in order to plug gaps in the German lines that were being inflicted by the continued British attacks. British high command eagerly envisioned that the tide was now shifting in their favour, that German resolve was collapsing and that a breakthrough was imminent. Nevertheless, German determination and organisation were hardly broken, and neither was their morale – or at least as much as the British high command hoped or imagined it would be. Renewed British attacks met only stiffer and stiffer resistance. The British always felt that the next big push would finally achieve the elusive breakthrough. Several times Haig had his division of cavalry ready to probe and expand the anticipated grand opening and rout the Germans, but the moment never arrived. Instead, both sides continued to pour ever more soldiers into the cauldron of intense fighting – temporarily gaining ground here and there, only to lose it back again in a pell-mell struggle.

The cost of ferociously contesting every wooded area, village, and point of high ground soon grew out of all proportion to the value of the territory being fought over. A point on the map became an end to itself, even if the point on the map was of no practical or tactical value. One such example was the Australian operation at

Pozières which, from the beginning of the battle in July, had been designated by the British command to be of essential tactical value and therefore the object of intense fighting. Finally secured by the third week of July, the destroyed village then endured a relentless pummelling by counter-attacking Germans, including a withering artillery barrage that rained down from surrounding ridges controlled by the Germans. Not until the first week of August did the Germans give up on the recapture of Pozières, reluctantly conceding control to the British. But this 'success' had required a month of punishing combat, with over 23,000 casualties in the taking of an objective that had been a primary goal of the British high command. For the newly deployed Australians, the Pozières episode had cost them more casualties in less than a month's fighting than in eight months fighting during the infamous Gallipoli disaster.

It was at this point in the campaign that Haig began to redefine his stated objective as to what the intense and remorseless carnage was designed to achieve: that breaking through was actually not an achievable goal, nor was it even imminently possible at this time. Instead, the Allied attacks were now deemed a process in wearing down the German army and forcing its future collapse and defeat through the method of attrition. Many have since labelled this as a course of 'mutual destruction' wherein the combatants would slug it out by the hundred thousand until there was only one man left standing. Certainly a case can be made for this argument and conclusion.

To this now declared end, the resumption of attacks continued on through the late summer and into autumn of 1916. By attacking German-held villages and strongpoints along the British front south of Thiepval, the Germans would be enticed into repeated counter-attacks, resulting in heavy casualties for each side, but which the Allies were better able to absorb. The village of Guillemont, near where the British and French armies joined, was finally secured by the British during the first week of September, provoking the largest German counter-attack of the battle. The French seized on this momentum and promptly mounted their largest attack, made in conjunction with the British push on the nearby village of Ginchy. The concentrated commitment of the German defenders to these positions, and the relative success of the combined Allied operation, produced mammoth casualties for the Germans as they desperately, and probably foolishly, fought to retain every foot of contested soil. The Germans endured 130,000 casualties during this prolonged period of Allied pressure on the southern sector, finally withdrawing to a more defensible position a mile to the rear. Once again however, the minor Allied gains, although succeeding on a relative basis, failed to allow for any sort of a breakthrough.

In mid-September, the British combined tank and infantry units for the first time and managed to capture the village of Flers, the first truly successful operation of combined infantry and mechanised forces, and a strong foretaste of the future of combined operations. Though only a few of the tanks were able to perform and survive the day, it did achieve the goal of securing Flers and pushing back the German defences a few hundred yards. By the end of September, the British position had been forwarded by 3,500 yards, and had obtained gains that had not been accomplished since mid-July. September's repeated counter-attacks had certainly devastated the German army, as it recorded its most costly month of casualties since the battle began. The Allies' overwhelming superiority in artillery, aeroplanes, tanks and troops were indeed wearing down the German army. Germany strained to maintain its endurance while coping with the distinct disadvantage of fighting a two-front war against the giant but awkward Russian army in the east and the combined Anglo-French army in the west. Germany's decision to 'bleed' the French at Verdun had turned into a costly drain on her own limited supplies and manpower, and the resulting lack of replacement soldiers and equipment for the Somme campaign was beginning to be painfully and felt.

At the end of September and into October, the British renewed their attention to the centre of the Somme sector at Thiepval, using General Herbert Gough's reserve Fifth Army to provide fresh soldiers for a vigorous series of attacks to capture Thiepval village and the surrounding high ground of Ancre Heights. The next six weeks would continue the Somme battle until cold and wet weather conditions ended the fighting in mid-November. Experimenting with a variety of techniques and approaches such as 'hurricane' bombardments (short and extremely intense artillery barrages followed by immediate infantry attacks), poison gas, dominant air superiority, creeping barrages (requiring accurate and experienced gunnery to place a curtain of artillery fire only a few hundred yards in front of an advancing infantry unit) and tanks enabled the British to finally take Thiepval and push on to capture the high ground around the Ancre Heights. Once again the Germans would put up stiff and resolute resistance for every village and redoubt, as positions changed hands back and forth through October and into early November. Casualties continued to mount as each side attempted to thwart the other's resolve through the willingness to extend the battle. Beaumont Hamel was finally overtaken, but the original objectives of Peronne in the south, Bapaume in the central sector and a breakthrough anywhere, were not achieved. By mid-November, with heavy weather setting in, the attacks by both the British and French ceased. German General Falkenhayn was relieved of command in late

Generals Paul von Hindenburg and Eric Ludendorff assumed command of the German army midway through 1916. Here they are conferring with the Kaiser. (Library of Congress)

August and replaced by the joint team of Generals Paul von Hindenburg and Eric Ludendorff, who would guide German strategy through to the end of the war.

A lull now set in on the Somme front that lasted over the winter. The Germans, under Ludendorff's direction, began preparing a new, stronger, sturdier and more defendable position several miles behind their current front lines. The German army retreated the following spring to this new so-called 'Hindenburg Line', abandoning the land that had been so heavily fought over during the previous six months of intense and horrific fighting. The British Army now occupied by default what had been virtually impossible to capture by force at the expense of 500,000 casualties. By the same token, the Germans were now willing to concede the property that they had so vigorously defended, and at a similar cost

The Thiepval Memorial is located in the centre of the Somme battlefield. Unveiled in 1932, it was designed by Edwin Lutyens and has inscribed upon it the names of over 72,000 Commonwealth soldiers whose bodies were never recovered. (Author's collection)

of between 450,000–600,000 casualties. But the Allies' original July objectives of Bapaume and Peronne, at 8 and 20 miles away from the initial Anglo-French lines respectively, remained in German hands.

8

TECHNOLOGICAL INNOVATIONS

The lethal and unrewarding slog that was the Battle of the Somme demanded some sort of alternative in either tactics or equipment, or both. In fact, the Somme saw the implementation of several technical developments that in the future would transcend the waging of war. Unfortunately for those continuing to plod through the nearly five months long battle, the improvements did not come soon enough or in great enough degree to affect a seemingly unending battle of ferocious and appalling attrition. By mid-August and into September 1916, the implication of a 'war of attrition' was beginning to be better understood by those in both France and Britain. It certainly emphasised the necessity for more food, equipment, guns and ammunition, but also the excruciatingly painful expenditure of countless human lives squandered on questionable targets of debatable value. The strategy demanded casualties to be endured on a massive scale in order to produce and increase the enemy's casualties on an equal if not greater scale. The British high command was now preaching the same doctrine as that set forth by the Germans at Verdun. Politicians in London, lower and upper line officers, as well as the ordinary trench-bound soldier began to recognise the futility in the seemingly suicidal assaults that continued unabated through the summer of 1916. Many began to question seriously the wisdom of such a policy and to seek viable alternatives.

Examples of the questioning were wide-ranging. In government, Prime Minister David Lloyd George, who personally attempted to rein in Haig and his arguably senseless attacks, called Haig a 'dunce'[20] and his method of waging war, 'a dismal narrative of military ineptitude'.[21] Winston Churchill, who had served for several months in the trenches of the Somme as a battalion commander of the 6th Royal Scots Fusiliers shortly before the battle began, vocally decried Haig's tactics. He is 'openly very hostile to me' bewailed Haig of Churchill's criticisms.[22] So pronounced and frequent were these criticisms during and after the battle that Haig was nearly removed after less than a year into his promotion, only to

Above left: David Lloyd George, Liberal British Prime Minister (1916–22), former Director of Munitions, and leader of the British government that brought victory to the Allied cause. Lloyd George was always sceptical of General Haig and British military high command, and he frequently clashed with their decisions during the First World War. Lloyd George represented Great Britain at the Versailles Peace Conference in 1919 and demonstrated a determination in the war effort that prior PM Herbert Asquith was perceived as lacking. (Library of Congress)

Above right: Winston Churchill served as First Lord of the Navy, Major (later promoted to Lieutenant-Colonel) of a battalion on the Western Front, and later as Minister of Munitions during the First World War. He was an early advocate of tanks as a means to break the stalemate on the Western Front. He also suffered considerable damage to his reputation by his advocacy of the Gallipoli Campaign, leading to his resignation as First Lord and returning as an active soldier and battalion commander. (Library of Congress, Bain Collection)

be saved by his good connections with George V and the upper echelon of the British Army, as well as the unavailability of a plausible replacement candidate. So too was the lack of an alternative strategy to break the stalemate.

This becomes further evident when reviewing similarly recorded examples. One corps commander's plea was made, not out of cowardice, but out of exhaustion and frustration in November 1916, near the Somme's frustrating conclusion. Lord Cavan, commander of the British XIV Corps, challenged an order to attack an extremely well-defended position at Le Transloy on 5 November in assistance of the French stationed beside his right flank. Cavan expressed his 'readiness to sacrifice … rather than jeopardise the French … but I feel I am bound to ask if this is the intention? For a sacrifice it must be'.[23] Cavan appealed to his commander, General Rawlinson, who upon examining the situation concurred that the attack was impossible and would be fruitless. However, upon consultation with French General Foch, Haig reversed the conclusion of Cavan and Rawlinson and ordered

Airplanes also became important during the First World War, initially for observation and later as a tactical weapon. Their importance increased as their numbers increased. Pictured here is French aviator Jules Védrines with his warplane. (Library of Congress, Bain Collection)

the attack to be carried out. The attack was duly made and XIV Corps suffered over 2,000 casualties. To no one's surprise, neither tactical gain nor observable contribution to the French position resulted from the sacrifice.

Situations such as these desperately encouraged changes: in thinking, in operation, in equipment and in method. Aerial warfare, poison gas and the tank all were introduced and developed during the First World War. The aeroplane began the war as a scout plane – an observer in the sky – but it soon evolved into a combat weapon. By the Battle of the Somme, planes played a vital role in observation and begun to have a more significant role in tactical operation. In fact, the British and French dominated the skies over the Somme during the summer of 1916, but were unable to take advantage due to the prevailing weather conditions of frequent heavy rains and low cloud cover. Poison gas, introduced by the Germans at Ypres in 1915, retained a reputation for its terrifying nature and nightmarish lethality, constituting as much a psychological threat as opposed to a decisive battlefield instrument.

Many other ideas and improvements to previous weapons began to make their appearance as each side sought to end the stagnation of the trench dilemma. Light submachine guns were introduced in a variety of forms, sizes and calibres, suitable for operation by a single soldier or in teams of two. These 'trench-sweepers' were developed as personal automatic weapons in order to increase the average

GAS

Poison gas, although used initially by the Germans, was quickly adopted by both the British and French armies, and delivered by distant artillery. Its unpredictable nature due to wind and weather conditions made it a treacherous and frequently undependable weapon.

The initial gas used was chlorine gas, which caused severe breathing problems and congestion in the lungs and throat; later phosgene gas was developed, which was even more poisonous. Inhaling chlorine gas could be fatal, but breathing phosgene gas would cause the victim to violently cough or choke to death. The most effective gas was mustard gas, a chemical agent causing severe burning of the skin, eyes, and breathing tract. It was not necessarily lethal, but it was extremely painful and debilitating. Mustard gas would not be introduced until 1917.

German soldiers, all wearing gas masks, crossing no man's land through a cloud of poisonous gas. Chlorine, phosgene, and mustard gas were used by both sides during the First World War. (Author's collection)

soldier's individual fire power. To be effective the soldier had to reach the opponent's trench, and it was only later in the war that they became commonly available. To be truly useful, these automatic weapons required corresponding tactical skills to fully take advantage of their effectiveness. The flamethrower, although dangerous to its user, also began to appear as a means to clear out bunkers and pillboxes. Combined with Mills bombs and hand grenades, the idea was to give each individual more killing power once he reached an opponent's defensive position. The problem remained, however, of getting safely across no man's land in the first place in order to inflict this enhanced killing power of the personal weapons possessed by the individual soldier.

Enter the tank. First used at the Battle of the Somme, the name itself was a code word to account for its enormous size and hide its true purpose as a land machine weapon. Combining caterpillar-style tractor treads to force through mud, shell holes, barbed wire and ditches, its bulldozer-like tracks allowed the vehicle to cross the roughest terrain. Powered by an internal combustion engine, it could traverse distances at a relatively speedy and powerful rate. It was armoured in order to shield those inside it and those crouching and manoeuvring behind it. Finally, it was armed with machine guns and small cannon enabling it to project its own firepower as it crossed open fields. In large numbers it was hoped to be a battle-changing weapon that would clear an enemy and open gaps in well-fortified defences.

TANKS

Ernest Swinton, a British engineering officer, had been appalled by the conditions and moribund philosophy of the trench war being conducted in France. He soon convinced the Imperial Defence Committee in London of a scheme to produce 'landships' of great size, power, and mobility to cross no man's land in order to break the stalemate of the trenches.[24] The result was the Mark I tank, a behemoth weighing in at 31 tons, with a crew of one officer and eight operators, and featuring four machine guns and two six-pound cannon. It could only travel at 3.5 miles per hour, but it was heavily armoured and could cross the most battered and shell-wracked terrain while trampling barbed wire emplacements with impunity. The name 'tank' is derived from the huge crates that the vehicles were shipped in – only a water tank could have been of such size and shape.

British tanks, first known as 'landships', were first used in August 1916 at the Somme. Though effective, they did not achieve a tactical or strategic breakthrough. (Library of Congress)

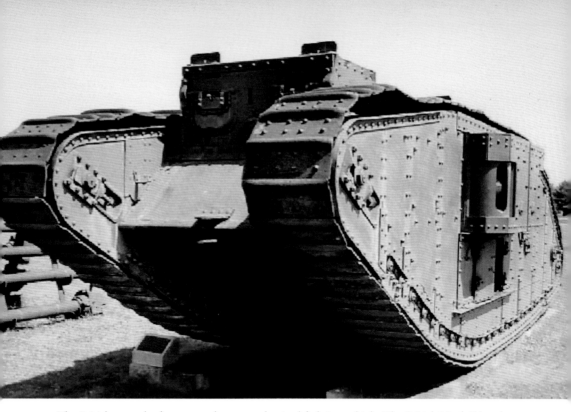

The British were the first to produce a mechanised fighting vehicle. The British Mark IV tank featured small cannon and machine guns with a crew of eight. Two types, curiously deemed 'male' and 'female' featured different arrangements of cannon and machine gun. (Author's collection)

General Haig embraced the development of tanks, and insisted on their participation during the Battle of the Somme. Unfortunately, there were too few of them and their dependability was poor. But it was a glimpse into the future of modern warfare and of things to come. Generals Haig and Rawlinson witnessed a demonstration of their suitability in early September of 1916 and both concluded that the available tanks needed further refinement and their crews more training. However, so desperate for some positive achievement in the course of the long drawn-out battle, Haig ordered their immediate use. Fifty-nine tanks were available and parcelled out to several divisions over several miles of front, fulfilling a role as a 'shock' weapon, but thereby diminishing their concentrated striking power. There were also no tanks held in reserve to follow on any successful penetration of German lines. In the event, ten tanks broke down before the assault began on 15 September and only nine were able to remain in service for the entire day, the rest breaking down or being disabled by either terrain or German guns. However, four tanks managed to surround and capture the tiny village of Flers—the first victory for the new weapon and an important harbinger of the future.

9

THE END OF THE BATTLE

Summer and autumn rains had turned the Somme battlefield into a quagmire of mud and waterlogged trenches. The pockmarked earth was a cratered moonscape of shell holes, torn earth, wrecked villages and denuded forests. Moving to and from the front was a nightmare in itself; artillery shellfire ranged from intermittent to ceaseless, and attempting to deliver adequate quantities of food, water, ammunition, equipment and replacements was an exercise in danger and horror. Traversing any part of the front, let alone attacking across no man's land, was in itself physically challenging due to the rutted and swampy conditions. Not only was human fatigue setting in but so too was equipment showing the strain of several months' constant action. British artillery had been used to such an extreme that, lacking periodic re-lining and repair, shells would occasionally fall short onto friendly lines, and occasionally worn out cannon, in desperate need of maintenance or replacement, sometimes exploded at the breech, killing and maiming entire gun crews. The soldiers, the equipment, the very ground itself, were all suffering the toll of the relentless endeavour.

British trench conditions were poor, with only the frequent rotation of units to the back lines providing availability to bathing and relief from lice. Decaying bodies attracted flies and overgrown rats, drawn to the unlimited supply of food, and created a fetid stench. Soldier's feet were constantly inspected for 'trench foot', a common malady caused by the damp environment. Control of sewage was a constant challenge and intestinal illness and flu was common. Along with the endless mud, this presented miserable, unhealthy and uncomfortable conditions for the ordinary soldier.

Assaults by the British continued into November in the face of cold, sleet and appalling conditions for both supply and advance. The commander of the XIV Corps reported to General Rawlinson on 5 November that, 'No one who has not visited the front trenches can really know the state of exhaustion to which the men are reduced. All of my General and Staff Officers agree that [the conditions]

Lice were a constant problem to soldiers living in the mud and filth of the trenches. Here, German soldiers being disinfected for lice. (Library of Congress, Bain Collection)

are the worst they have seen, owing to the enormous distance of the carry of all munitions – such as food, water and ammunition.'[25]

The summer's steady rainfall had produced oceans of mud to impede and hamper the fighting, but it took the onset of cold and snow to limit the movement of essential supplies to the front to the point where renewed assaults were halted. So it was not the casualties, or lack of tactical gains, or the failure of strategic success that finally encouraged Haig to call off the battle and hunker down into secure lines for the upcoming winter. Allied high command met at Compiègne and decided to put a halt to further offensive operations on the Somme front. November's snow and freezing temperatures would undermine any rational attempt to carry on the battle; 18 November marked the last of the Allied attacks.

Historian Denis Winter points out how, from July to November, 'the British and German armies fire thirty million shells at each other and suffer a million casualties between them in an area just seven miles square' in order to barely move the front forward a few miles.[26] Historian A. J. P. Taylor commented how, 'Strategically, the battle of the Somme was an unredeemed defeat … The enthusiastic volunteers were enthusiastic no longer. They had lost faith in their cause, their leaders, in everything except loyalty to their fighting comrades. The war ceased to have a purpose. It went on for its own sake, as a contest of endurance.[27] This last comment alone would have probably pleased General Haig, as he had adjusted the battle's goal to that of a battle of attrition. So too would he have probably been pleased with the soldiers' willingness to fight on for the good of their comrades – something they and another fresh army of several million soldiers would be required to do for the next two years.

10

CONCLUSIONS

The Somme Battle did not achieve the desired breakthrough originally predicted and avidly sought by General Haig and the Allied high command. Instead it proved a stalemate of the most severe variety, that of relentless fighting and killing – total self-destruction waged on an unprecedented size and scale. In four months of fighting the Allies had gone forward roughly 7 miles but had fallen several miles short of their pronounced goals of Bapaume and Peronne. However, to France's great relief, the German pressure on Verdun had been relieved and the German offensive staunched. Furthermore, during the two great Western Front encounters of 1916, Verdun and the Somme, the German army had suffered nearly 1 million casualties. Although the Allies suffered a similar loss, they remained confident that victory could be achieved through a war of attrition. Assuming continued Russian and Italian survival – and that was not a foregone conclusion – the Anglo-French army commanders calculated that the struggle could be over perhaps in 1917, or surely by 1918. The Allies would prevail due to their larger number of soldiers and greater capacity for material support. This proved to be true.

The Allies also held onto the belief that German morale was faltering and with that the German willingness to fight would be broken. This certainly proved to be false. However, the British Royal Navy's increasingly effective blockade of the German ports was gradually strangling the German economy. Germany's inability to import food and resources was by now a serious component in Allied strategic thinking, leading to the conclusion that it was only a matter of time before the Allies would be able to achieve victory and force Germany to surrender.

To achieve this end, many challenges would need to be overcome. For the British, another 'new' army would have to be raised, this one a conscript army of between 1 and 2 million men, in order to replace the two armies that had been virtually destroyed during the first three years of the war.[28] New techniques of operational warfare would need to be developed, practised and exercised, incorporating and integrating greater numbers and use of planes and tanks. Most importantly, victory

The remains of trenches still found on the Somme battlefield. This is the sector occupied by units from Newfoundland at Beaumont-Hamel, site today of some of the best preserved, century old trench lines. (Author's collection)

on the battlefield would require recognition of the importance of overwhelming artillery support. To dominate a battlefield, artillery would require to accurate pinpointing of in-depth targets as well as targets that were out of sight. New and better ranging methods, aerial observation, sound and flash readings and greater coordination between infantry and artillery would all enable attacking ground units to 'bite and hold' positions during offensives. Mastering counter-artillery barrage techniques would then prevent ensuing counter-attacks and artillery fire from repeatedly undoing what successful assaults had achieved. These skills would need to be sharpened through training and experience. Production of artillery barrels, shells, timers and high-explosive munitions would need to be increased and improved to ensure fewer duds. All of these technical issues would need to be resolved in order for the Allies to progress in their war of attrition.

The Germans, under their new leadership command of Paul von Hindenburg and Eric Ludendorff, spent 1917 consolidating their defences and remodelling their strategy. In the east, Russia surrendered after the Bolshevik Revolution. The world witnessed an entirely new set of power dynamics as the Lenin-led Bolshevik government concluded a separate peace with Germany – the Treaty of Brest-Litovsk. Germany was able to shift over 1 million soldiers from the Eastern Front to the Western Front, completely off-setting the projected manpower and morale benefits that the Allies imagined they had been gaining through their war of attrition.

Generals Hindenburg and Ludendorff became virtual leaders of Germany as the war progressed, committing Germany to their unrestricted submarine policy. (Library of Congress, Bain Collection)

Germany also resumed unrestricted submarine warfare against Allied merchant shipping in the Atlantic Ocean, in an all-out bid to starve out the British and force their submission through either a surrender or negotiated settlement. The hope for British withdrawal from her continental commitment would thereby guarantee a virtual victory for Germany over France. This was a costly gamble for the Germans, and one that would inevitably defeat them.

Unrestricted submarine warfare drew the sleeping giant of the United States into the conflict on the side of the Allies. In terms of material and financial resources, potential military manpower and industrial output, this provided an overwhelming advantage to the Allies. None of these factors were minor; from increased naval power to combat the submarine threat, to hard cash, to the US willingness to raise an army of several million men and send them to France – all helped to tip the balance in favour of the Allies. The United States entered the war with an enthusiasm of international optimism to conclude a war 'to end all wars'. Fresh soldiers took a year to be raised and trained, but they began pouring into France by early 1917 with confidence. Most important to the Allied strategy of attrition was that they arrived in large numbers.

In 1917, the French, under their new supreme commander General Robert Nivelle (Joseph Joffre being shunted aside after the failure of the Somme), engaged in a series of diabolically suicidal attacks, against the better judgment of prior experience and all common sense. The 1917 Nivelle offensive resulted in disaster. On all levels it set new standards in failure: tactically, numerically and, most dangerous of all, in the collapse of French army morale. Another 200,000 French soldiers became casualties, with nearly 30,000 killed, in a hopeless and senseless offensive to again attempt a breakthrough along the Western Front. This offensive led to a mutiny, whereby numerous divisions of French soldiers were willing to defend their lines but would no longer participate in suicidal attacks of dubious consequence and chances for success. Perhaps as many as fifty-four divisions were affected and there were an estimated 20,000 desertions. This mutiny resulted in the execution of forty to sixty mutineers and the imprisonment of many more. It eventually passed, but the damage to morale and French strategy was near fatal. The Germans would never learn of this mutiny, and it would be weeks until even the British high command became aware. The philosophy of French *élan* and the power of the 'will and the spirit of the offensive' was now bankrupt. The repercussions to French battlefield tactics were not overcome until near the war's end.

By the spring of 1918 the Germans, under Generals Hindenburg and Ludendorff – now virtual co-leaders of Germany, were willing to double down on their risky submarine gamble with an all-out Western Front offensive and make a supreme bid for victory before the waves of American soldiers began to arrive. Using newer combined operations techniques, hurricane artillery barrages and smaller probing penetration units that could establish small breakthroughs which led to larger breakouts, the Germans launched a series of attacks to sever the British line into half and prove that the war would not be won in the trenches. The British were pushed into a retreat that General Haig would blame on his former friend General Gough, who was subsequently sacked. Once again, the British and French, now with American support, were challenged to hold off the German advance within 50 miles of Paris at the Second Battle of the Marne. It was a second near-miss for the Germans, allowing them to again almost win the war – and just ahead of the arriving American army that would soon begin pouring into Europe at the rate of 250,000 soldiers a month.

The near-defeat convinced the Allies that they needed one supreme commander to oversee strategy and supervise operations. In the spring of 1918 French General Ferdinand Foch was appointed Supreme Commander of the Allied Armies, and it was Foch who led the combined armies to victory on the Western Front. Following their failed spring 1918 offensive, the Germans discovered themselves spent and vulnerable. The Allies launched their own massive counter-punch in mid-summer 1918. This Allied offensive featured overwhelming superiority in artillery, tanks, aircraft, manpower and material. The Allied armies then embarked on their own war-winning drive to push back the German army right to the German border. A beleaguered Germany finally requested negotiation for an armistice followed by their reluctant concession of defeat. The Allies would eventually prevail.

So the question remains: was the Battle of the Somme successful, or even necessary, to the ultimate outcome and victory of the Allies? Even German General Ludendorff admitted that the Somme had 'annihilated the cream of the German army', and 'a battle such as the Somme could not be fought again by the Germans in their current state and allow the war effort to survive'. Was the Somme offensive, and the ensuing war of attrition, the reason this ultimate Allied victory was achieved? If you accept the point of view of historians such as John Terraine, then the answer is yes – overwhelmingly. The argument by Terraine, among others, calls for praising Haig and his strategy, and congratulates him as the author of the final victory. Haig, according to Terraine, can be faulted for some of his mistakes, but his approach was correct. If on the other hand you accept the version of history

The 'Big Four' Allied leaders at the Paris Peace Conference in 1919 that officially ended the First World War. From left to right: Prime Minister David Lloyd George of Great Britain, Prime Minister Vittorio Orlando of Italy, Prime Minister Georges Clemenceau of France and President Woodrow Wilson of the United States. The treaty produced a controversial result which provoked widespread animosity in Germany eventually leading to the Second World War. (Library of Congress, Bain Collection)

as presented by historian Denis Winter and others, then Haig remains the butcher who only impeded, delayed and exacerbated a bad situation into a terrible carnage of unnecessary slaughter, and that, despite the gross errors and failings of Haig and his team of commanders, the Allies managed to achieve victory. In this school of thought, the war was lengthened and made unnecessarily worse and more costly by the wanton waste of human life as reflected in needless battles such as the Somme. Winter and other observers accuse Haig and his cohorts of a complete lack of imagination and a dull stubbornness in the face of repeated failure, faulting their inability to comprehend the staggering depth of their obsessive commitment, repeatedly ordering men to their death with endless offensives that produced no meaningful gain. Somewhere in-between we find American historian Gerard DeGroot with probably the most accurately balanced assessment, 'Though he [Haig] was the architect of victory, there were flaws in his design.'[29]

The two schools of thought concerning Haig's tactics have provoked endless debate that rages on. Certainly, the Allies won the war and the wearing down of the Germans was an essential element. Yet, if Haig's subsequent battles are any indication of his imagination and credibility, then his methods must be severely questioned when considering his willingness to launch another six month offensive during the 1917 Passchendaele campaign (Third Battle of Ypres), producing yet another frightful round of casualties. 240,000 British soldiers, with perhaps as many as 50,000 killed, became victims of the unabated assaults through the filth and mud of the rain-soaked battleground. British wartime Prime Minister David Lloyd George later wrote of Haig and the campaign, 'Passchendaele was indeed one of the greatest disasters of the war ... No soldier of any intelligence defends this campaign.'[30] Haig had preferred to attack in Belgium at Passchendaele rather than the Somme in 1916, and one year later Passchendaele again placed Haig's tactics on display. Arguments about Haig's strategy remain unresolved to this day with vehement opponents on each side. Certainly the death tolls at the Somme and Passchendaele are shameful, and there was no great victory at either site. Nor once again was there any real gain in tactical or territorial achievement to justify the casualties. But the British did improve and perfect their ability to fight, and once again the Germans were severely worn down. In November 1918 the allies would achieve their victory and Haig would be praised and rewarded for his leadership by many, but no one can deny the horrible conditions and the monstrous casualties of that victory.

A point of agreement by all historians and observers, however, is the courage of the brave soldiers of the British Army. Their courage has never been questioned, nor has their willingness to do as they were commanded.

Above: British soldiers behind their sandbagged trench. Their bayonets are mounted on their Lee Enfield .303 rifles, the standard issue weapon in the British Army. (Library of Congress, Bain Collection)

Below: German soldiers in their trenches. (Library of Congress, Bain Collection)

11

ANALYSIS

One hundred years later, it seems easier to discern what went wrong on 1 July 1916, and why the following four and a half months of destructive and horrific fighting and killing seems so futile and unnecessary to our modern eye. Hindsight, as they say, is 20/20. Could things have been different? Were certain individuals to blame more than others? Was the Somme a waste of over half a million Allied soldiers for absolutely no beneficial gain? These are difficult questions. The main answer is that First World War engaged European powers possessed of incredible wealth and resources, with seemingly limitless quantities of manpower, to fight a modern twentieth-century war and provide for the vast appetite of such an industrialised encounter of devastation; and that once embarked upon, the war took on its own logic. Once engaged, Europe could not, or at least would not, withdraw until one side or the other either collapsed or surrendered. The war took on a life all of its own. This is the most basic fact which must be remembered, even if the entry into the war was a 'mistake' and the method of waging the war approaching criminal. So too must be remembered the wholehearted enthusiasm that the populations of these nations displayed at the war's outset. The excited eagerness to enlist in 1914 by every opposing nation cannot be ignored.

The struggle on the Somme was an extension of this disastrous encounter between monumental great powers locked in conflict. It took the culmination of modern industrialised warfare in size, technology, futility and catastrophic death to determine what we now acknowledge as unresolved goals. The arguments about the Somme's significance, necessity and result have been contested for the last century. What it did and did not accomplish, and why it became the battle that ensued, are great questions – and not easily answered.

Certainly as a 'battle' the Somme did not accomplish a breakthrough and end the First World War. Nor was it a 'victory' in the sense of a battlefield victory for either side. If the Allied goal was to achieve a victory by breaking through the German lines, then it was a failure. In terms of territory or military objective, both strategically and tactically nothing was gained on the battlefield. Even in the optimistic sense of the British gaining ground, or in the German case by holding ground, then it would be still be considered at best a hollow victory.

Only when placed under the umbrella of the later claims by Haig and other Allied leaders, that the battle was fought in terms of an intentional and larger 'war of attrition', and for the desired whittling away of German soldiers, supplies and morale, could it possibly be considered a positive and necessary step toward the road to victory. For this route to achieve success, two more years of bitter attrition would yet be required. Only after the German request for an armistice and its reluctant surrender, and later the Treaty of Versailles confirming total surrender and forced admission of guilt for the start of the war, would this strategy take on any purchase of credibility. But the price for that 'victory' would be the greater catastrophe of planting the seeds for the Second World War, and the world-shattering events that the First World War precipitated.

The view today looking across no man's land toward the German lines from Thiepval in the centre of the British offensive. (Author's collection)

If one accepts the argument and the rationale for the Battle of the Somme being intentionally fought as a centrepiece in the war of attrition, was the price paid by the Allies too great? Or even necessary? Could the Allies merely have fired the same massive amounts of artillery for a week and feigned an attack, then repeated the supposed preliminary action again every month until November, but cleverly doing nothing in the way of assaults in order to achieve the same effect without the staggering casualties of 'going over the top'? Was the repeated use of massed infantry assaults not only impractical, but completely unnecessary? Certainly the Somme, in its brutality and lethality, achieved several things, even if at an enormous cost in human life.

Therefore, did the Somme campaign achieve its goals?

1. Yes, for pressure on Verdun lifted. The German commitment to its goal of bleeding France to death at Verdun had been reversed until it was the Germans instead who were haemorrhaging under the relentless Allied pressure at the Somme. Haig and his supporters, however, would respond that it was only through repeated assaults. But the burden on Verdun was reduced and allowed the French army to hold the line.

2. No, because there was no breakthrough to victory or the seizure of important tactical positions. Territorially the Allies had not achieved a breakthrough or gained any significant ground. On the contrary, they had advanced only approximately 7 miles over a battlefield that stretched more than 15 miles. This penetration came at the expense of nearly two-thirds of a million casualties. Ironically, the ground so desperately fought over, plus another roughly 15 miles more, would be conceded by the Germans in April 1917 when the Germans withdrew to their more heavily fortified and shortened 'Hindenburg' line.

3. Perhaps, as it allowed in the long run for the deterioration of the German army through attrition. German General Ludendorff himself concluded that, after the Somme, 'the German army was exhausted' and that the German army could not sustain another battle such as the Somme.[31] And to this end Germany was forced to either sue now for peace, or to alter her war strategy. She chose the latter, recognising Britain as her greatest foe, and resumed unrestricted submarine warfare in an effort to starve them out. However, this brought the United States into the war, tipping the balance in both material and manpower to the Allies, and dooming Germany to defeat. So in fact, even though a terribly tragic human sacrifice, in the aftermath of the Somme the Germans were forced to alter their strategy and eventually concede and capitulate in surrender.

Ludendorff's conclusions, however, run headlong into the numerical facts of battlefield casualty ratios. In sheer numbers, the Germans were far better at killing the Allies than the Allies were at killing Germans. The statistics give credence to the justification that, even though the Allies won the war, the Germans maintained a superiority in terms of killing, rather than being killed.[32] So what happened? The Germans were fighting three separate wars: against the numerically stronger Russians on the Eastern Front, helping the Austrians on the Italian front, and confronting the Anglo-French coalition on the Western Front. Despite their efficiency, it proved too much for them to endure. The Allies, whether we condone it or not, championed the war of attrition, even if the cost was to be paid in the inhumane spilling of blood – man for man. The Allies, with greater manpower, could better afford this cost than the Germans. The way the war was fought was reduced down to which side could best sustain and tolerate the cost in both treasure and blood and, significantly, in will.

With the surrender of Russia in the spring of 1917, the Germans were able to briefly obtain the upper hand and wage a near war-winning offensive in the spring

Ulster Tower and Chapel near Thiepval. A rare successful attack on 1 July was able to pierce the German lines north of Albert on the Somme battlefield. Despite achieving their objective, due to a lack of support the Irish unit was forced to withdraw by the end of the day. (Author's collection)

of 1918. However, it failed. The Allies, reinforced with American troops, were able to hold off the Germans, turn the tide, and within six months defeat the depleted, demoralised and materially inferior German army on the battlefield, and force Germany's hand to peace. The war would not be won in the trenches but with the new tactics of combined operations. Tanks, aircraft and better tactical methods developed and learnt throughout the years of war, were wedded together with superior manpower and industrial output. As painfully slow and lethal as this process proved to be, it was how gunners would perfect their creeping barrages and how commanders would now train and use smaller attacking groups to probe and prepare a sector for assault. When future offensives were launched, it would be under a volcanic rain of artillery, both before and during the assault. Advancing soldiers would be shielded behind a curtain of falling artillery shells, while longer range artillery with pinpoint accuracy would block any reinforcing units from counter-attacking.

These methods would be developed both tactically and technologically by trial and error and through experience, but the pity of it all was the price in human life that had to be paid in the learning process. The Somme campaign was a tragic part of the price.

Whether it was for their king, their nation, or their fellow 'pals', the British soldiers at the Somme displayed incredible courage and resolve in an attempt which in all probability could not have been accomplished at that time and in that place. To the Germans and their relentless counter-attacks in the face of incessant Allied assaults, so too their spirit and courage never wavered in holding the contested ground that the Allies were so intent upon seizing. It was a struggle of titans, using industrial-age weapons of power and destruction like never before. To this end both sides were extremely successful.

Some commanders fared better than others, and there is much criticism to go around, but it is often too easy and tempting for us today to look back and demonise what was or was not done. Each side trusted those who led them to the predicament in which they found themselves ensnared. It is to this fact that so many millions were let down by a disturbing lack of military imagination and the moral courage to question the abominable tactics repeatedly employed. Whatever the enduring legacy of the Somme and the First World War, the only actions that we can never doubt is the sacrifice, courage and determination of those that 'went over the top' on 1 July 1916.

Above: The Bertangles German cemetery at Fricourt, France, at the Somme battlefield. These stones represent mass burials of German soldiers. (Author's collection)

Below: British soldiers in a front line trench during the Battle of the Somme. (Courtesy of Jonathan Reeve)

WHAT NEXT?

BOOKS

Carver, Michael, editor. *The War Lords*, Weidenfeld and Nicholson (1976)

Cuttell, Barry, *One Day On the Somme*, GMS Enterprises (1998)

David, Saul, *Military Blunders*, Carroll and Graf (1997)

DeGroot, Gerard, *Christian Science Monitor* (article) (2014)

Dooley, William G. Jr., *Great Weapons of First World War*, Army Times Publishing (1969)

Ferguson, Niall, *The Pity of War*, Penguin (1998)

Gilbert, Martin, *The Somme*, Henry Holt (2006)

Hart, Peter, *The First World War*, Oxford University Press (2013)

Hart, Peter, *The Somme*, Pegasus (2008)

Holmes, Richard, *The Western Front*, BBC Books (1999)

Johnson, J. H., *Stalemate!*, Arms and Armour Press (1995)

Jones, Archer, *The Art of War in the Western World*, Oxford University Press (1987)

Jorgensen, Christopher, editor, *Great Battles*, Parragon Publishing (2007)

Keegan, John, *The Face of Battle*, Penguin (1976)

Keegan, John, *The First World War*, Alfred A. Knopf (1998)

Macdonald, Lynn, *Somme*, Penguin (1983)

Macksey, Kenneth, *Technology in War*, Prentice Hall (1986)

Marshall, S.L.A., *First World War*, American Heritage (1964)

Middlebrook, Martin, *The First Day On the Somme*, Penguin (1971)

Neiberg, Michael S., *The Western Front 1914-1916*, Amber Books (2008)

O'Shea, Stephen, *Back to the Front*, Avon Books (1996)

Parker, Robert J., *British Prime Ministers*, Amberley (2011)

Ross, Stewart, *War in the Trenches*, Wayland Publishers (1990)

Winter, Denis, *Haig's Command*, Penguin (1991)

Winter, Denis, *Death's Men*, Penguin (1978)

TV/VIDEO

'World War 1 in Colour', 2003, narrated by Kenneth Branagh

'First World War, the Complete Story (CBS)', 1963, narrated by Robert Ryan

'Battle of the Somme' 1916, (silent), Pathe

'The Story of the Somme', 2005

FILMS

'The Somme', 1927

'The Trench' 1999

'The Somme' 2005

'The Somme – from Defeat to Victory', 2006

NOTES

1. Grey, Viscount, *Twenty-Five Years*, 1892–1916 (London, 1925) p. 25
2. Keegan, John, *The Face of Battle* (London, 1976) p. 217
3. David, Saul, *Military Blunders* (New York, 1997) p. 95
4. Gilbert, Martin, *The Somme* (New York, 2006) pp. 164, 192, 244
5. Homes, Richard, *The Western Front* (London, 1999) pp. 139–40
6. Keegan, p. 238
7. David, p. 101
8. Holmes, p. 138
9. DeGroot, Gerard. *The Christian Science Monitor*, Article, May 2014, p. 27
10. Johnson, J. H. *Stalemate* (London, 1995) p. 60
11. David, p. 103.
12. David, p. 103 (citing John Keegan)
13. David, p. 102
14. David, pp. 102–3
15. Middlebrook, Martin, *The First Day on the Somme* (London, 1971) p. 157
16. Hamilton, R. G. A., *War Diary of the Master of Belhaven, 1914-1918* (London, 1924)
17. David, pp. 106–7
18. Carver, Michael (ed.) *War Lords* (London, 1976) p. 36; Johnson, p. 73
19. Holmes, p. 147
20. Neiberg, Michael, *The Western Front 1914–1916* (London 2008) p. 189
21. Ross, Stewart, *War In the Trenches* (New York, 1991) p. 47
22. Neiberg, p. 189
23. Holmes, p. 154
24. Keegan, John, *The First World War* (New York, 1999) p. 297
25. Johnson, p. 84
26. O'Shea, Stephen, *Back to the Front* (New York, 1996), p. 88 (citing Denis Winter)
27. David, pp. 107–8 (citing A. J. P. Taylor)
28. Marshall, S. L. A. *First World War* (New York, 1964) p. 242
29. Johnson, p. 20. (citing Gerard DeGroot)
30. Terraine, John, *The Road to Passchendaele. The Flanders Offensive, 1917* (London, 1977) pp. XIX-XX
31. Holmes, p. 152
32. Ferguson, Niall, *The Pity of War* (London, 1998) pp. 292–4

INDEX

Allenby, General Henry 38
Ancre River and Heights 11, 23, 37, 39, 68
Asquith, Herbert 6, 14, 72

Bapaume, France 10–11, 36–7, 39, 70, 80
Barbed wire 22, 38, 40–1, 48–50, 57, 61–2, 75
Beaumont-Hamel, France 37, 39, 59–60, 68, 81
Below, General Fritz von 31–2, 65
Bite and hold (tactic) 29–30, 39, 47, 81
Blenk, Karl (German soldier) 61
Brest-Litovsk, Treaty of 81
British Expeditionary Force (BEF) 9, 26–8

Cavan, Lord (General Rudolph Lambart) Commander of British XIV Corps 72, 78
Cavalry 30–1, 66
Chantilly, France 9, 26, 36
Chipilly, France 55
Churchill, Winston 15, 71–2
Contalmaison, France 64
Creeping barrage (tactic) 33, 68, 91
Crimean War 17

Falkenhayn, General Erich von 30–2, 65–6, 69
Fayolle, General Emile 33
Flamethrower 75
Flers, France 10, 68, 77
Foch, General Ferdinand 11, 33–4. 72. 83
Franco-Prussian War 9, 19
Franz Ferdinand, Archduke 9, 19
French, General Sir John 9, 24, 28–9
Fricourt, France 10, 37, 39, 42, 63

Gallipoli Campaign 67, 72

Gallwitz, General Max von 31
George V, King 29, 72
Ginchy, France 10, 67
Gommecourt, France 37-38
Gough, General Sir Hubert 31, 33, 68, 83
Grey, Sir Edward 17
Guillemont, France 10, 67

Haig, General Sir Douglas 6, 9, 11, 23–4, 26, 29–30, 32–4, 38–9, 50, 64–7, 71–2, 77, 79–80, 83–85, 88–9
Hamilton, R. G. A. 62
High explosive 24, 28, 36, 41, 43, 81
Hindenburg, General Paul von 32, 69, 81–3
Hindenburg Line 69, 89
Howitzer 35, 39–40, 42, 53
Hurricane bombardment 68, 83

Joffre, General Joseph 26, 28, 33, 50, 65, 82

Kitchener, Lord Horatio 5, 16, 27–8, 50
Kitchener's Army 27

La Boiselle, France (Lochnager Crater) 37, 39, 45
Le Transloy, France 11, 72
Lloyd George, David 6, 14, 71–2, 84–5
Ludendorff, General Erich 32, 69, 81–4, 89–90

Machine gun 22, 35–6, 38, 41, 44, 57, 75, 77
Mametz, France 10, 37, 39, 42, 63
Marne, (First and Second) Battle of the 33, 83
Micheler, General Joseph 33
Mills bomb (hand grenade) 47, 50, 75

Moltke, General Helmuth von 54
Montauban, France 10, 37–9, 63
Mortar 35, 40, 44
Mutiny (French) 43, 83

Nivelle, General Robert 43, 82–3

PALS (volunteers) 16, 28, 62, 91
Peronne, France 10–11, 68, 70, 80
Pétain, General Phillipe 50–1
Picardy, France 5, 23
Poison gas 68, 73–4
Pozières, France 10, 37, 39, 67

Rawlinson, General Sir Henry 29–30, 34, 38–9, 64, 72, 77–8
Rupprecht, Bavarian Crown Prince 31

Sarajevo, Bosnia 19
Schlieffen Plan 19–21, 54
Schwaben Redoubt 10–11, 63
Serre, France 29, 64
Shrapnel 40–1, 57
Submarine (warfare) 82-83, 89
Swinton, General Sir Ernest 75

Tank 33, 68, 73, 75–6, 91
Territorial Force 27
Thiepval, France 10–11, 37, 39, 65–8, 70, 88, 90
Tyne Cot Cemetery 8

Verdun, Battle of 9–10, 15, 23, 26, 28, 30–2, 35–6, 39, 50–1, 65, 68, 71, 80, 89
Versailles, Treaty of 11, 72, 84, 88
Voie Sacrée (Sacred Way) 51

Wilhelm II, Kaiser 9, 15, 54, 69

Ypres (Battles of Ypres and Passchendaele) 8, 28–9, 73, 85